Wicked
ST. AUGUSTINE

Wicked
St. Augustine

Ann Colby

THE
History
PRESS

Published by The History Press
Charleston, SC
www.historypress.com

Copyright © 2020 by Ann E. Colby
All rights reserved

First published 2020

Manufactured in the United States

ISBN 9781467145374

Library of Congress Control Number: 2019951989

CONTENTS

PREFACE

Wicked St. Augustine is different from most kinds of history books about St. Augustine on the bookshelves. I wanted to tell readers about prostitution, bootlegging and gambling, all of which played significant roles in the city from the day it was founded in 1565. Surprisingly, this part of the story of St. Augustine, the nation's oldest continuously occupied city, has not been told to date.

When I first started this venture and reached out to sources for factual research on the trifecta of moral sins in the Oldest City, I was met with a lot of skepticism—because, after all, nothing as sordid as prostitution, gambling or the production and sale of illegal liquor could ever have been prominent or important factors in the city's history. St. Augustine is a *family* town. The heroic actions of the early colonists and the Catholic Church fill its history books. The bravery, contributions and influence of the settlers brought to Florida's shores in 1768 from the Spanish island of Menorca continue to this very day. The great works of Henry Flagler, which remain part of his legacy, are the basis of St. Augustine's economy even today.

Over the years, St. Augustine was a military town, a seaport and, yes, a tourist town. All of these endeavors ensure that prostitution, alcohol sale and consumption and gambling would be main sources of livelihood for at least a portion of the population and desirable entertainment for even more. Today, New Orleans documents the history of its brothels, madams, taverns and casinos with a certain amount of civic pride. A large chunk of the city's income is derived from the tours, lectures and exhibits based on those professions, not to mention the millions the Big Easy rakes in every year from alcohol sales and legalized gambling. Since St. Augustine predates New Orleans by over one hundred years, surely it has its own story to tell.

This book digs below the surface of St. Augustine's unacknowledged underground. Direct documentary evidence is scarce. I had to piece it together from crumbling court records, city directories, ancient property deeds and scratchy disintegrating oral history tapes (which must be digitized before their remarkable disclosures about St. Augustine history are lost forever). Some material came from the firsthand memories of longtime St. Augustine residents; other information emerged from the previous research of local historians to whom I am ever indebted. With this book, I hope that these once hidden subjects will become an official part of St. Augustine history so that the women and men who supplied the city with its "sinful delights" will be remembered for what they accomplished for themselves and their community.

Of course, I hope the reader is entertained. That is the best way to learn history and to remember it.

ACKNOWLEDGEMENTS

This book would not have been written without the assistance and knowledge of Charles Tingley, Robert Nawrocki, Chad Germany and Claire Barnewolt at the St. Augustine Historical Society Research Library. Without them, I would still be wondering where to start, given the dearth of documented material on vice in St. Augustine. They pointed me in directions I would never have thought to take and gave me insights into St. Augustine history that led to surprising consequences for my personal research. I thank them all.

To Carol Busby (J.B.K.), a writer of supreme talent in the field of historical fiction, who encouraged me every step of the way, who edited and re-edited, who made suggestions for improvements all throughout the process and who was there to just sit and listen when the going got tough and the inspiration dried up. Thank you, my dear, and M.T. thanks you as well.

To my husband, Bill MacLeod, and my daughter, Logan Slaughter, for putting up with my endless babbling about my research, the ladies and the story I wanted to tell. And for putting up with the hours and hours I spent secluded in my world of research and writing. I think I am finally back.

To the Dead Poet Society, Breezeway Alliance, who sat through innumerable dinners listening to tales of Blanche Altavilla and the ladies of West Augustine. Sorry for the repetition, but at least you ate well.

And finally, to the St. Augustine miscreants themselves. To Blanche Altavilla, Ocie Martin, Margaret Norris, Billie Bird, Margaret Darling, the Masters family, the Mickler family, the Canova family, the Hugas family, the Pacetti family and all the other St. Augustinians whose private and public lives I probed in detail. I was entranced by both your strengths and your foibles. I celebrate them all. Thank you for sharing them. I will not forget.

A NOTE ON HENRY FLAGLER

*A*ny discussion of the history of St. Augustine, including the history of its "shady ladies," its high-rollers and the many men and women who supplied the city with thousands of gallons of the "water of life" during the county dry periods and during Prohibition, must include mention of Henry Flagler. An industrialist and Rockefeller business partner, Flagler began his development of St. Augustine in 1883 as the crown jewel in a string of resorts he built down the east coast of Florida along the route of his Florida East Coast Railway.

His declared goal for St. Augustine was to create a "Newport of the South," a haven during the winter months for the rich and those who aspired to wealth of Flaglerian proportions. Flagler believed that if he built the right properties, his desired clientele would flock to them. So build them he did: three luxury hotels, all the facilities and utilities necessary to support them and both roads and railroads to reach them.

He didn't stop there. He acquired newspapers and publicity outlets to control the public perception of his new resort, built churches to cement his moral reputation in the community and worked tirelessly to generate the image of a family-friendly Florida vacation playground long before Walt Disney did the same for Central Florida. Flagler's efforts still bear fruit today. St. Augustine continues to protect and maintain its reputation as a tourist destination for families, featuring entertainments that are history- and education-oriented, with the added attractions of its pristine beaches, parks and nature preserves.

Henry Flagler sitting beside his railroad. *St. Augustine Historical Society.*

But we also have Henry Flagler to thank for St. Augustine's Golden Age of Wickedness. Prior to Flagler's entry on the scene, sleepy little St. Augustine had the usual share of women for rent, unlicensed liquor and penny ante wagering, beginning from the first day of its founding in 1565. Nothing much for a visitor to write home about. Then came Flagler with his grandiose plans and his fabulously wealthy friends. In just a few years' time, St. Augustine went from a small, dusty backwater with some crumbling Spanish buildings of vague historical interest to the winter haven for the richest families in the eastern and midwestern United States. Flagler, a staunch Presbyterian and teetotaler, wanted the city he was building to have a spotless moral reputation, so St. Augustine enacted its first laws regulating immoral activities. Brothels were declared illegal, as were the sale of unlicensed alcoholic beverages and participation in games of chance.

On the surface, St. Augustine became the squeaky-clean environment Henry Flagler needed to market to his uptown northern crowd. But he was no fool, and neither were the local entrepreneurs, who saw the influx of affluent tourists pouring into the Flagler hotels as guaranteed money in their bank accounts. Money demands opportunities to spend it, and big money multiplies those opportunities tenfold. Flagler's male guests needed non-spousal female companionship, so the brothels grew in number, size and luxury and the landladies prospered. Gambling has always been a pastime for all socioeconomic classes. In Flagler's St. Augustine, it became part of daily life, with opulent clubs for the wealthy where millions of dollars changed hands. But there were more modest meeting rooms designated for the locals and less wealthy to wager smaller amounts on games of chance. All of these facilities were well known to the public and to law enforcement. All of them prospered.

As for liquor, Flagler may not have imbibed, but everyone else in St. Augustine did, with prodigious capacity. All of the Flagler properties served alcohol, even when the city and county were dry. If open sale was illegal, then the liquor—locally made or imported and bonded—flowed in private "clubs" anyone (other than minors or women) could join for a modest fee, entitling "the member" to purchase as many intoxicating beverages as his cash flow would allow.

Ultimately, permitting "wicked" activities to grow, organize and prosper benefitted Henry Flagler's bottom line. Despite the public persona of

The Ponce de Leon Hotel (Flagler College) as it appears today. *Author's collection.*

moral uprightness he created for both himself and his newly reborn city, sin flourished, with his silent blessing and, in some cases, assistance. The Flagler double standard on wickedness in St. Augustine extended for many decades beyond his death. He may not have wanted to be remembered for that, but we thank him for it all the same.

1
HOW IT ALL BEGAN

St. Augustine did not begin its history in a state of sanctity, as much as that was desired by the Catholic Church. It was a settlement of soldiers, sailors, churchmen and average men and women looking for a new start in a new world. Those men and women brought with them the skills and trades needed for survival in the harsh environment that was La Florida.

The new colony was founded on September 7, 1565, by Pedro Menéndez de Avilés and his group of colonists after sailing from Cadiz, Spain. Menéndez's list of necessary tradespeople for his new colony included carpenters, tailors, weavers, bakers, rope and weapons manufacturers, cobblers, washerwomen, fishermen, hunters, armorers, stockmen, pitch makers, Indian traders and charcoal burners. He also brought with these essential personnel the seeds for other industries that would thrive in St. Augustine: a master brewer for the production of alcoholic beverages, tavernkeepers, boardinghouse keepers, various gaming implements and even a complement of prostitutes. Menéndez was a realist.

The master brewer, listed on Menéndez's cargo manifest, would have been an artisan essential to the success of the colony. Alcoholic beverages, from beer and wine to spirits, cordials and liqueurs, were consumed by everyone—and not just as sacramental wine or sailor's grog. Having a steady supply of quality drinkables ensured both the health and happiness of the colonists, especially necessary in the extreme heat and humidity of

Pedro Menéndez de Avilés, founder of St. Augustine. *St. Augustine Historical Society.*

their new surroundings. Beer provided necessary hydration without the risk associated with untreated water.

Archaeological digs in the areas of first colonization have shown that despite the hardships the colonists endured, they still had their leisure time and entertainments. Fragments of dominos, dice and gaming pieces have been recovered, leading to the belief that wagering wasn't far behind. By the time the young colony was a mere fifteen years old, gambling—with cards and dice—is mentioned in the city records as taking place at private homes, in the guardroom at the fort and in the several taverns that had sprung up throughout the town.

The first official mention of prostitution in the records of St. Augustine occurred in April 1566. A soldier of Menéndez's company was reprimanded for giving a prostitute a gift of cloth, openly, at the town well. His sin was not in consorting with her. After all, a man needed the comfort of a woman in those difficult times, and the woman in question was likely present in the colony for that purpose. His mistake was that he gave her a gift, an expensive one, and acknowledged her in front of the entire colony, which was not acceptable under the social rules in effect.

So it has been through much of the history of St. Augustine. The prostitutes, the brothels they lived in and the madams (self-titled "landladies" by the nineteenth century) who managed their careers, the producers and consumers of alcohol and the gamblers, both high stakes and low, have always existed in the city and its environs. Though largely unacknowledged in the history books, the newspaper accounts, the travel magazines and everywhere else "polite" society resides and records its accounts of day-to-day life and events, they thrived nonetheless.

The roles that these miscreants played in St. Augustine are largely revealed through secondary sources such as maps, census counts, archaeological documentation and military or court records. Occasionally, there are direct references—a quote in a newspaper, a mention in a personal journal, a quick quip in a neighborhood gazette—but these are rare. What emerged from a Holmesian set of clues sprinkled throughout the documentation left in recorded St. Augustine history was that prostitution, the brothels and the landladies who supported the industry, the bootleggers and the gamblers were a thriving part of its economy for centuries. As such, they merit inclusion in any chronicle of St. Augustine life. Names from the powerful families of Spanish and Menorcan heritage appear in records documenting "wickedness" in the city along with those of ordinary citizens. In later years, these professions touched the very best of St. Augustine society as fashioned and nurtured under the watchful eye and influence of Henry Flagler. Far from being sordid, underground, criminal enterprises, in St. Augustine these businesses were largely open, well-known and countenanced by the city fathers—and occasionally by the city mothers as well.

In St. Augustine's first days as a settlement and Spanish colony, prostitutes plied their trade as individuals, probably brought by Menéndez as essential service providers for his soldiers and sailors, who, by order of the king of Spain, were forbidden to marry in the New World. Consorting with indigenous women was discouraged, if not actually forbidden, as dangerous to the delicate diplomatic relations between the Spanish and the native residents, although such relationships did form. As the colony grew and flourished, a town grid formed with residences for the townspeople, business sites for tradesmen and, in abundance, taverns.

For much of the city's history, taverns were not only centers for relaxation and entertainment but also places where business was discussed; politics formed, dismantled and reformed; and decisions were made that guided the fate of the colony. A review of the earliest of St. Augustine city maps shows that for many decades of the first Spanish and the British periods, taverns vastly outnumbered any other type of commercial establishment in the city.

In those days, the business plan for a tavern was radically different from our modern concept as a location where one goes to obtain alcoholic beverages and occasionally food. In early St. Augustine, most forms of masculine entertainment were available in taverns—not only food and alcoholic beverages but also gambling and women hired for sex, under the guise of offering "boardinghouse" services. The taverns provided a relatively safe and convenient location for the business of prostitution, for both the women who provided the service and the men who purchased it. So while the lower floor of the building provided space for the sale of food and drink, the upstairs was reserved for the sale of sex and for stakes gambling—although gambling also took place on the lower floors as well.

St. Augustine's best existing example of this classical tavern structure is its Oldest House, which is located across from the military barracks at 14 St. Francis Street. The Gonzalez-Alvarez House, as it is known, was originally constructed in the first Spanish period, then modified as it changed owners during the British, Second Spanish and American periods. Its most celebrated owners were Joseph Peavett and Maria Evans—during the British and second Spanish periods—who turned their home into the tavern/gambling/boardinghouse seen throughout St. Augustine's history. No doubt they capitalized on the proximity of the military barracks across the street; large numbers of soldiers guaranteed a steady income from gambling and the sale of alcohol and women.

By the time St. Augustine had existed for one hundred years, the portion of the city grid bounded by the City Gates on the north, Bay Street (now Avenida Menendez) on the east, Treasury Street on the south and Tolomato Street (now Cordova) on the west showed the existence of at least forty taverns, most of which likely also provided space for prostitution and gambling. They were St. Augustine's first brothels, a welcome distraction for the soldiers, sailors and fishermen who constituted the bulk of St. Augustine's male population in those years.

The Catholic Church does not appear to have openly condemned what was surely taking place nightly in the taverns of the city. No records describe assaults on such practices from the pulpit or from those who determined what laws governed the young colony, who would have been highly influenced by the church. Prostitution and gambling, in their own way, contributed to the peace and order of the community, essential in such dangerous times.

The Oldest House, St. Frances Street, circa 1930. *St. Augustine Historical Society.*

The Oldest House, St. Francis Street, as it appears today. *Author's collection.*

Prostitution also served as an economic benefit, giving women who would have otherwise been destitute and a burden on the colony an income and means with which to contribute to the colony's resources.

This is not to say that the taverns were always the source of peaceful camaraderie in St. Augustine. They weren't. As the city grew in its importance as a seaport (importing, among other commodities, large amounts of liquor produced in the West Indies and Cuba), the soldiers and sailors constituting the bulk of the male population often turned the taverns into locations for what might be termed "vigorous dispute settlement." Accounts abound in St. Augustine records of conflicts over the outcome of card and dice games, usually fueled by alcohol, resulting in stabbings, beatings and deaths. At one point, the city considered minimizing the violence by banning sailors from possessing knives within the city limits, but this idea was quickly stricken by the sailors, who argued that carrying a blade in their profession often made the difference between life and death—and not just in taverns.

Gambling disagreements were not the only source of tavern violence in St. Augustine. Women were just as often the point of contention, be it competition for the affections of a particularly comely lass working the upstairs precincts of the tavern or a slight, real or imagined, to the reputation of one's wife. Again, the records are rife with tales of blood spilled over women, often resulting in the death of one or more of the participants in the quarrel and occasionally in the wounding or death of the woman herself. Unfairly, if the authorities made arrests in these situations, it was usually the woman at the source of the conflict who received the severest punishment, without regard as to whether or not she physically participated in the brawl that initiated the arrests.

Prior to the American period, the local authorities tended to treat tavern fracases as minor incidents, punished by short-term incarceration and/or a fine, unless the injury or death occurred to a local, in which case the incident was taken much more seriously. Once St. Augustine was ceded to the United States in 1821, legislation with regard to the sale of alcohol and women and of operation of gambling houses got a bit more serious, in that the Americans had figured out that there was money to be made—not from prohibiting these activities, but from taxing them six ways to Sunday.

TO MAKE ROME HOWL

Why the Oldest Profession Flourished in the Oldest City

When considering the question of prostitution from the perspective of morality, society has traditionally seen prostitutes and landladies as purveyors of sin and evil, luring men from their homes and families to breach the Ten Commandments in a manner that breaks down the carefully ordered structure of society. Throughout St. Augustine's history, there were periods when prostitution was publicly condemned and, at least on the surface, efforts were made to stop or slow its proliferation.

These efforts usually coincided with a change of governor or, after coming under American jurisdiction, during periods immediately before and after local elections. Ironically, during the late nineteenth and early twentieth centuries, when organized prostitution was at its peak, news about the industry was fanatically suppressed by Henry Flagler, who owned the local newspapers and who wanted no blot on the careful image of the "Newport of the South" that he had created. On the rare occasions that prostitution was mentioned, it was always in the context of moral outrage or, as one municipal court judge commented for the *St. Augustine Herald* in August 1899, the numerous brothels in the city "simply make Rome howl and nights hideous." Yet there were always women available to run the sex industry and men to avail themselves of those services.

Why did women in St. Augustine become prostitutes and landladies? In general and in public they were accused of being immoral—so overwhelmed by lust and greed that they chose this occupation as an outlet for their vices. This, of course, disregards the role played by men in providing the market for their services. But history and the legal system tell a much more complicated story. The real reason prostitution existed and women chose it as an occupation has always been economic.

Beginning with the first Spanish period in St. Augustine and continuing for decades thereafter, women were subject to their father's or a brother's decisions until they were married. Upon marriage, women were dependent upon the will of their husbands. Women could engage in legal transactions and testify in court only with the permission of their husbands, fathers or brothers. Under Spanish law, women were able to inherit and hold property left to them by their parents. This property could not be seized for the debts of their husbands. All other property inherited or acquired by a married woman came under the control of her husband and could be dispersed as he saw fit. Once a woman was widowed, however, Spanish law allowed her to engage in legal transactions and redress grievances in court in her own right. She was also entitled to one-half of her husband's estate. Unfortunately, this legal emancipation also meant she was liable for any debts her deceased husband may have left behind.

Today, by act of law and by changing perceptions of what women are capable of accomplishing, both mentally and physically, almost all occupations are open to women. During the Spanish and British periods in St. Augustine, women were limited in what they could legally do to earn a living. A woman could grow and sell food, weave cloth, cook, do laundry, serve as a seamstress, care for the children of other women or provide midwifery skills to the community. Of these occupations, only midwifery and fine sewing were open to women of the middle and upper classes—anything else brought severe social disapproval and ostracism.

As often happens in a community where the primary male occupations are military or fishing-related—carrying a higher-than-normal fatality rate—there were a disproportionate number of widows in St. Augustine. In this growing Catholic community, many of these widows were left with a substantial number of minor children to support. Records of the first Spanish period are riddled with accounts of widows of soldiers petitioning the Spanish crown for their deceased husbands' military pension, which was provided for under the "Plaza Muerta." The crown established this "dead pay" as one of the first official social welfare programs in the New World.

Unfortunately, it usually took a minimum of two years for the petition process to wind its way through the Spanish government—two years during which, unless she had a well-to-do supportive family, a widow and her children might starve to death. Even when a widow had been approved to receive the monies due her under the Plaza Muerta, bureaucratic delays and the vagaries of shipping to the colonies often meant that pension payments did not arrive quickly. This left many widows deeply in debt from borrowing against anticipated pension funds.

Because many of these women were considered middle-class, they could not work in the lower-class trades to get out of debt. If a family were wealthy enough to own their own home or other substantial building at the time the husband died, the widow might take in boarders or operate a part of the building as a tavern. Another common solution to the problem, judging from Spanish pension records, was for the widow to become the mistress of another man. Under Spanish law, a concubine or recognized mistress had a legal right to support of her and her children of the relationship. Furthermore, the children had the right to be legally recognized by their father—although they did not have an automatic right to inherit from him. In a classic catch-22, however, if a woman entered into such a relationship to keep herself and her children from destitution, she was subject to having the military pension to which she was entitled denied on the grounds of her immorality for engaging in prostitution.

In some instances, the local St. Augustine governor chose to assist widows by granting them temporary pensions from the city treasury. The temporary pension for the widow of a common soldier was approximately 547 reales per year, a single reale being worth about $0.06 in today's money. Cost of living estimates for the period suggest that a family with two children might live sufficiently on an annual income between 616 and 950 reales. Even with the grant of a temporary pension, a widow and her children would still find living difficult, with destitution and starvation still a looming reality.

By the end of the second Spanish period and the arrival of the Americans, the status of single women and widows with children—indeed the status of all women—took a steep downturn. Under American rule, women's control over their own lives diminished, when many of the rights they had under Spanish law were rescinded. A single woman remained under the jurisdiction of the males in her life without emancipation. The right to conduct legal affairs on her own behalf, to contract in her own name and to control her own inheritance disappeared. Only widows retained a semblance of the right of a woman to make her own decisions and control her own life.

The social programs established by the Spanish government for the support of widows and their children ceased to exist, replaced largely by what funds could be raised through the volunteer efforts of charitable religious organizations. This type of assistance was haphazard at best, and distribution was complicated by the fact that it was usually given only to those women deemed worthy in the eyes of the organization raising and distributing the funds.

Under increasing economic pressure, the number of brothels in St. Augustine and the number of women staffing them grew. Once St. Augustine came under American jurisdiction, the number of taverns in the city decreased and brothels moved out of taverns and became independent establishments, often operating under the sobriquet of "female boardinghouse." These "boardinghouses" often incorporated gambling rooms and the sale of liquor into their services offered. By the mid- to late 1800s, the city maps show these houses on Spanish Street, Tolomato Street, Cuna Street, Marine Street, Oneida Street, Washington Street and Hospital (now Aviles) Street. The highest concentration was on Charlotte Street, both to the north and south of King Street. In 1881, for the first time and probably in recognition of the impending revitalization by Henry Flagler, the City of St. Augustine passed an ordinance outlawing the operation of houses of ill fame and gaming, though the ordinance was rarely enforced. By 1900, more and more women were looking to prostitution as a means of acquiring independence, money and property, even relocating to St. Augustine from the large cities in the North because of the opportunities St. Augustine provided.

With the advent of Henry Flagler's hotels and a flock of wealthy new customers, prostitution in St. Augustine became a successful economic venture working hand in hand with the political forces that decried its existence in public while patronizing, encouraging and funding it in private. Women who were part of that venture prospered in what was otherwise a man's world because of their business acumen. It wasn't until the late 1950s and early 1960s that the combination of increased women's rights and the advent of the sexual revolution tolled the death knell for organized "respectable" prostitution in St. Augustine.

THE NOTORIOUS AND SUCCESSFUL LANDLADIES

*O*n the evening of April 21, 1892, two women and two men were arrested on West King Street in the city of New Augustine, later incorporated into the city of St. Augustine and today known as West Augustine. One of the women, Blanche Travis, was charged with "keeping a lewd house." Lily Hendricks, also known as Helen Hendricks, and the two men, Ferd Traver and Joseph Appler, both deputy sheriffs for St. Johns County, Florida, were charged under an ordinance that directed the arrest of all "the tenants, boarders, or visitors of said premises" (a bawdy house). All four were brought to trial four days later, April 25, 1892, in the Mayor's Court for the City of New Augustine.

The trial record is the only one in early St. Augustine court records that transcribes word for word what happened in an arrest and trial for operating a brothel. The transcript gives some interesting insights into how brothels were regarded at the time. Blanche, Lily, Ferd and Joseph were arrested by William Hernandez, a St. Augustine police officer who had been appointed marshal of New Augustine by G.H. Spencer, the mayor of that city. Five temporary deputies aided in the arrests. John Sanchez, Frank Andreu, C.C. Andreu, John Burns and John Center accompanied Hernandez. Sanchez was a member of one of the oldest and most respected Heritage families in the area: their residency dates back to the original Menéndez colony. The marshal testified that "there was a great deal of indignation in the City of St. Augustine that day [the day of the arrest]" and he had been sent for by the mayor of St. Augustine and John Sanchez.

The two men gave him a warrant to serve on Blanche Travis and the occupants of her house and told him it was at the behest of certain prominent men in the community. Hernandez refused to disclose the names of these particular men, although counsel for the defense requested he do so, and his refusal was sustained by the court. Hernandez also refused to disclose whether or not he and these other unnamed men had conspired to arrest Blanche at other times as well or planned the current arrest without a complaint or prior to a warrant being issued. One of the other witnesses, a Mr. Gowell, however, testified that such threats to arrest Blanche had indeed been made and that she had been arrested previously on the same charge.

Hernandez and his deputies all testified that none of them had seen any activity in Blanche's house that evening that would give cause to believe that anything "lewd" was taking place on the premises, although Frank Andreu thought he had seen Ferd Traver walk upstairs with a red blanket in his arms. The key testimony against the accused came from Blanche's neighbor J.W. Cook, who testified that he lived 250 feet away from her house and that he could see "a great many persons in carriages and on foot going there night and day." He also complained of the constant noise coming from the house, from the carriage traffic, the music and the "cursing and swearing." From that, he concluded, Blanche's house earned the reputation of being a "lewd house," as the law defined it.

The defense called C.J. Perry, the sheriff of St. Johns County, who testified that he had taken Blanche into custody on the same charge on a county warrant requested by the unnamed "important" men on April 19, 1892, and pledged Blanche's security in lieu of a bond, allowing her to stay home until her discharge by order of the judge of the circuit court on April 22, 1892. Sheriff Perry also testified that he had ordered his deputies, Traver and Appler, to stay with Blanche until her case was discharged. Ferd Traver testified that he and Appler were indeed at Blanche's house on the night of April 21, as ordered by Sheriff Perry. He also revealed the presence at the house of another person, a boy, Phillip Manucy, who had not been arrested, presumably because he was a minor.

Traver also addressed the "indignation" in the city of St. Augustine the afternoon of the arrest. Traver said he had confronted William Hernandez in the circuit courthouse that afternoon and accused him of orchestrating the arrest that was coming that evening, saying he (Hernandez) said he was "coming to catch us all." Hernandez retorted that he didn't have the power to order that arrest, other men did. Another witness, J.J. Allen, was called to testify as to the conspiracy of "important men" to arrest Blanche, but the judge (who also was the mayor of New Augustine), refused to allow his testimony and struck the names of the men from the court record.

The verdict? All four were found guilty as charged. The two women were sentenced to serve five days each in the New Augustine jail, and the two men were fined five dollars, with their sentences suspended. The attorney for Blanche and Lily, A.J. Corbett, another prominent scion of St. Augustine, filed a bill of exceptions to the verdicts rendered by the mayor of New Augustine, and the cases were quietly dismissed in May. The names of the important men of St. Augustine who were apparently seeking to shut Blanche down? We will never know. And it seems that their efforts were in vain anyway.

The trial described earlier is an account of one of the many arrests of Blanche Altavilla, née Travis, as found in the court records for St. Johns County. Blanche operated brothels on West King Street in what was, for many of its years of operation, the town of New Augustine, called West Augustine after its absorption into the city of St. Augustine.

Blanche was arrested at least eleven times for a range of criminal activities related to the entertainment of men residing in and visiting St. Augustine: operating a house of ill fame, making and selling illegal liquors and running an illegal gambling operation, as well as operating boardinghouses and gaming rooms without a license. Notably, she was never convicted, and her biggest supporters were prominent judges and lawmen; in fact, they always personally posted her bail. Blanche's businesses were long-lived and stable. City records indicate that she was active in various capacities from approximately 1883 until 1953, when she died in St. Augustine at the age of ninety-three.

Blanche did not confine herself to illegal activities. Property records for St. Augustine and St. Johns County show that she owned large parcels of land in both St. Augustine and West Augustine, managed substantial blocks of land for absent owners and held mortgages on even more properties. Blanche's hand can be seen in many legal transactions through the first half of the twentieth century in St. Augustine, but she is rarely mentioned in the annals of the city's history. Perhaps her place in the development of St. Augustine would have had a greater degree of public acclaim if she had been male rather than female.

Blanche Travis arrived in St. Augustine in 1880 as an unmarried woman of twenty. Where she came from, how she got here and why she chose St. Augustine are mysteries, although we do know she was born in Marion, Ohio. Once she arrived, she sank deep roots and remained largely on her

Blanche Altavilla's Country Club on West King Street. *Author's collection.*

property on West King Street for her remaining seventy-three years. She acquired the land located at and around at 262 West King Street starting in 1883, purchasing the largest parcel in 1905. In 1911, she built the large house still located on the property. She eventually owned or controlled through mortgages all of the surrounding property bordering the streets called Travis Lane, Travis Place and Blanche Lane, all located in what is now known as the Altavilla subdivision.

On the lands surrounding her main house, known locally as the "Country Club," Blanche built a series of taverns where she sold her personally manufactured liquor, put in gambling facilities and even ran other brothels. One of the brothels was managed by one of Blanche's contemporaries, friend and part-time business manager Margaret Norris. Margaret was known as "Big Margaret" because of her stature, her deep, booming voice and, most strikingly, her enormous kindness and generosity to the poor of the New Augustine community. Big Margaret made sure that all leftover food from the Country Club and its environs was distributed to the hungry in the neighborhood. Even during the Great Depression, she continued

Margaret Norris's house as it appears today, at 266 West King Street. It adjoins Blanche Altavilla's house on the right. *Author's collection.*

this practice so that even in hard times, a good meal was always available to those who needed it.

Blanche's domain remained for many years an entertainment fixture in St. Augustine. According to the witness testimony contained in her 1892 trial for operating a lewd house, a constant stream of carriage and foot traffic moved down King Street at all hours of the day and night from St. Augustine to Blanche's Country Club. Likely many of Blanche's customers came from Flagler's resort hotels on King Street: the Ponce de Leon, the Alcazar and the Cordova.

Her popularity endured. Locals reminiscing about the World War II years in St. Augustine recalled cars full of soldiers from Camp Blanding in Clay County, Florida, lining West King Street, waiting their turn for entry into the precincts of the Country Club. The Country Club was even immortalized in fiction: Robert Wilder's novel *God Has a Long Face*, the story of a poor family building an empire in the wilderness of North Florida, has a lengthy account of one character's 1907 visit to St. Augustine to purchase a quantity of its excellent local bourbon and to seek solace in "the evil glitter of Babylon."

That Babylon is further described as discreet lanes off the main road (King Street) in West Augustine, just past the San Sebastián River. The lanes contain a succession of houses, mostly small bungalows—side by side and shaded by Spanish moss–draped oaks—where the girls plied their trade. The protagonist notices that the prostitutes proudly display their pink medical inspection certificates, issued monthly by a local doctor. Some of the girls were from local Menorcan families and provided a plentiful complimentary breakfast for their guests who committed to an overnight stay. This was organized and controlled prostitution in St. Augustine. This was the Country Club.

In 1909, when she was forty-nine years old, Blanche decided to marry. She chose as her husband Salvatore Altavilla, a twenty-four-year-old Italian immigrant who arrived in St. Augustine via New York City in 1908. Sam, as he was called, immigrated to the United States from Naples, Italy, at the age of twenty in 1905. He later became a citizen of the United States and served in the U.S. Army during World War I.

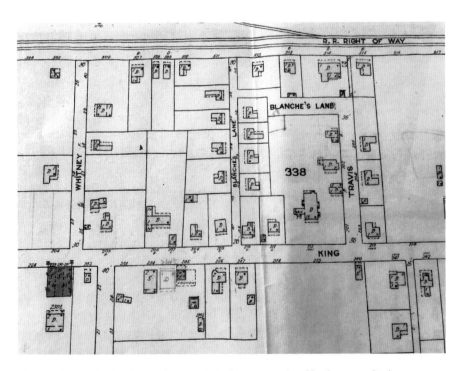

Blanche Altavilla's Country Club property in New Augustine. Her house and primary brothel is located in Block 338 at no. 212. Margaret Norris's house is located at no. 211. Map from the 1920s. *Property records, St. Johns County, Florida.*

During his short marriage to Blanche, Sam operated a garage and a tavern on Blanche's properties. After their divorce in 1916, he went on to work for the St. Augustine Transfer Company in several capacities, including chauffeur and cab driver. In 1920, Sam married Mayme Colee, daughter of James Colee, owner of the St. Augustine Transfer Company, which provided all carriage service, by horse and later by automobile, to the Flagler hotels.

By 1924, Sam and Mayme had moved into Blanche's residence at 262 West King Street. They remained in residence with Blanche, operating taverns, pool halls and gambling houses at the Country Club, with Sam specifically supervising the moonshine operation until his death in December 1950. After being widowed, Mayme continued to live with Blanche, managing a tavern, until Blanche's death in 1953. After Blanche's death, Mayme moved from 262 West King Street to an apartment complex built and owned by Blanche located at 229 West King Street. The occupants of Blanche's apartment complex, which was styled to look a bit like a miniature of Flagler's Ponce de Leon Hotel, with a Spanish tile roof and balconies, included a number of ladies who had formerly worked for Blanche at the Country Club. Maybe it was part of Blanche's retirement plan for her workers.

After her divorce from Sam Altavilla, Blanche called herself the "Widow Altavilla," despite the fact that her ex-husband and his new wife were living under her roof. The title gave her the financial and legal advantages of widowhood under American law. In all city and census records from 1924 until her death, Blanche remains the Widow Altavilla. This was not unusual in St. Augustine. In fact, most brothel landladies styled themselves as widows, notwithstanding their actual marital status, because of the legal improvements such status brought into their lives and businesses.

During her years of operation, Blanche was charged with at least eleven criminal offenses according to court records. Five of these charges were for operating a house of ill fame, three for making and selling illegal liquor, one for operating an illegal gambling hall, one for operating a gaming room with no license and one for operating a rooming house with no license. The opponents who demanded her arrests were always "certain important men" in St. Augustine, as noted in various warrants and transcripts. Their names were stricken from the court records to protect their privacy and reputations.

Blanche's allies included various St. Johns County sheriffs, deputy sheriffs and judges. In several of her arrests, it was the county sheriff who posted her bail and stood as her surety. What records exist show only one conviction, for operating a house of ill fame, and that conviction was appealed and later dismissed. All other charges filed against Blanche either resulted in outright dismissal by the judge or acquittal by all-male juries. No records show that Blanche ever served any time in jail or paid any court-levied fines during her long career.

Although Blanche's reputation was primarily based on her operation of brothels, she was nearly as well known for her success as a bootlegger. She made her own whiskey, which was aged and then stored in and served from coffee urns prominently displayed in the parlors of her houses or sold by the bottle to thirsty customers. Much to the delight of the children of St. Augustine, Blanche conducted a side business with them, buying all the glass bottles they could collect and paying them the princely sum of five cents per bottle.

Although it is difficult to determine precisely, the level of influence Blanche Altavilla had in St. Augustine during her years of operation appears to have been substantial. Clues sprinkled throughout city property and civil court records show numerous sales and transfers of property involving Blanche, in both the city of St. Augustine and in New Augustine, as well as many foreclosure suits and satisfactions on properties for which she held the mortgages. Blanche also appears to be at the center of a well-organized assemblage of the city landladies. She either outright owned the land on which their brothels were located or, in the case of Ocie Martin, the prominent Lincolnville landlady, held the mortgages on her properties.

St. Augustine records show a pattern of novice landladies, after initial arrests for operating houses of ill fame in locations all over the city, relocating within the year to Blanche's Country Club block. There they continued to ply their trade, forming an area akin to the contemporaneous and infamous Storyville district of New Orleans, albeit with less violent crime. Among those charged with operating brothels in either St. Augustine or New Augustine and then relocating to the Country Club after arrest were Doris Shaw, Annie Wynn, Marie de Medici (who, along with her husband, Paul de Medici, operated a brothel at the corner of West King Street and what is now South Leonardi Street) and May Harrell.

Blanche's supremacy among the landladies of St. Augustine may have been aided by a coincidence of history. She was a contemporary of and from the same hometown (Marion, Ohio) as the twenty-ninth president of the United States, Warren G. Harding. Harding, known for his pursuit of leisure, particularly in the forms of golf and womanizing, was a frequent visitor to St. Augustine for over twenty-five years, both before and after he ascended to the presidency. He often held court in his special suite at the Ponce de Leon Hotel. He patronized St. Augustine's golf courses with great regularity and was known to mingle with the locals in evenings on the town. It is not hard to imagine Harding also taking in the delights of St. Augustine's renowned brothels and other masculine entertainments, especially when some of them were being proffered by a girl from his own hometown.

Court records of the day clearly show cooperation between the landladies, with Blanche as their unofficial head. When Blanche sought her divorce from Sam Altavilla in 1916, she did so with the assistance of Margaret Norris, Marie de Medici and Ocie Martin. Margaret Norris testified as to Sam's infidelity and Blanche's efforts to be a proper wife. Ocie Martin provided both the locations (her house at 80 Park Place and one of the Charlotte Street brothels) and the girl with whom Sam was allegedly sporting, Elizabeth Armstrong. Marie de Medici added information about an additional infidelity, with a woman named Nell Reidstine who apparently also worked as a prostitute. And as late as 1942, Blanche, Norris and other landladies operating in the County Club block served as witnesses in a civil hearing over corruption in the St. Augustine Police Department. At the time of that hearing, eighty-two-year-old Blanche still actively participated in her business interests.

By the early 1950s, when she reached her nineties, Blanche was still a woman who made one sit up and take notice. A woman who worked as a teller at the Bank of St. Augustine in those days stated that every Monday morning, Blanche would come to the bank, dressed elegantly in the most stylish fashions, to deposit large amounts of cash in varying denominations. She recalled that Blanche was certainly "the most fashionable woman I had ever seen in St. Augustine."

On April 28, 1953, Blanche died of a heart attack at her home on West King Street. In her last will and testament, she left her entire estate to her good friend and attorney, Bertram Mickler, with one condition: that he purchase for her a suitable, tasteful stone to mark her gravesite. Blanche was buried a few days after her death, on a Thursday afternoon, at Evergreen Cemetery. Reverend George Downs, the pastor of Calvary Baptist Church, officiated. As Blanche wished, her grave is marked by a simple stone engraved with her name, her date of death and the ubiquitous "Rest in Peace." But to the end, she was a woman of quality—all the surrounding grave markers are granite, while Blanche's is marble.

While Blanche Altavilla was operating her successful brothels on West King, another equally successful landlady managed trade in Lincolnville, the black section of town. Ocie Martin arrived in 1908, shortly after her June 1908 marriage to Charlie Martin, a St. Augustine resident. Ocie, in

Left: Blanche Altavilla's grave in Evergreen Cemetery, St. Augustine, Florida. *Author's collection.*

Below: Portrait of Ocie Martin in front of her Park Place house, by Richard Twine. *St. Augustine Historical Research Library Collection.*

her youth called Ossie Mitchell, hailed from Palatka, Florida, just west of St. Augustine on the other side of the St. Johns River. She and Charlie, who worked at various bars and pool halls on Washington Street, took up residence at 80 Park Place in Lincolnville.

The marriage was short-lived. In October 1910, Charlie abandoned Ocie to take up with other women in Lincolnville. Shortly after his departure, court records show Ocie being indicted for assaulting Charlie with the intent to commit murder, although the records do not show that she was ever tried or convicted. This could be because on the day of the assault, Ocie caught Charlie in bed with a married woman of her acquaintance, a Rosa Clark. By the standards of the time, this was plenty of provocation for trying to shoot him. In January 1913, Ocie filed for divorce from Charlie, alleging adultery, physical and mental abuse and citing that he repeatedly called her a prostitute and was profane and obscene toward her. Her divorce was granted, although Ocie had to pay all costs for the proceedings. It is noted in the city census records that Ocie thereafter styled herself as the Widow Martin until her death on December 30, 1933. Like Blanche, she understood the benefits of widowhood.

She continued to reside at the Park Place address, which she solely owned. Ocie then acquired additional properties at 80 Bridge Street in Lincolnville and on North U.S. 1 just outside of the city where she operated brothels, taverns and restaurants. These properties appear to have been partially financed from mortgages taken out on the Park Place property—mortgages held by Blanche Altavilla.

The Widow Martin was a colorful character. Children in the neighborhood were warned to stay away from her home on Park Place, lest they be tempted by the frequent sound of jazz music coming from the musicians who played there in her spacious parlor. She was a handsome woman—photographed on several occasions by the celebrated Lincolnville artist Richard Twine—known for her beautiful contralto voice and for her penchant of carrying her pet parrot with her when she was out and about in town. Oral histories of St. Augustine credit her with operating extremely successful brothels. Her girls, mostly of mixed race and imported from New York City, were said to be the prettiest in the city. Ocie made annual recruiting trips to New York to acquire her girls, insisting that all candidates be healthy, cultured, stylish and mannered. Several noted portraits of attractive young women, names unknown, were taken by Richard Twine on Ocie Martin's front porch and in her front yard at the Park Place residence. Likely they were also employed by her.

Portrait of an unidentified woman in front of Ocie Martin's Park Place house, by Richard Twine. *St. Augustine Historical Research Library Collection.*

According to accounts from bellhops employed at the Alcazar Hotel during the first quarter of the twentieth century in St. Augustine, many of Blanche's and Ocie's customers came from the Flagler hotels. Customers made their requests for female companionship through the bellhops at the hotels, who would then, depending on the type of girl requested, contact the appropriate landlady to complete the arrangements. The bellhops interviewed noted with much delight that their salary for a six-day work week, at twelve hours each day, averaged five dollars per week. The landladies, on the other hand, paid them between three and five dollars per girl solicited—a far more lucrative employment incentive.

Ocie continued her monopoly on the trade in women of color in St. Augustine until her death in her early forties from kidney failure and erysipelas (a skin infection) in 1933. From all accounts, she lived her life to the fullest and in the process became one of the city's best known and most successful businesswomen.

Blanche and Ocie were by no means St. Augustine's only thriving landladies. Margaret Darling and her husband, Jack Darling, operated establishments across the street from each other on Sanford Street, while Marie and Paul de Medici kept a thriving house on West King Street in New Augustine. The de Medicis also operated a successful meat and grocery mart in New Augustine, supplementing their brothel income (or vice versa). Among Ocie Martin's competition in Lincolnville were Sarah Burke, who ran a brothel at 35 Marine Street, and Ida Walton, a black woman court records show was fined five dollars for running a brothel in the area. Unfortunately, the records do not state the address of her business.

It is interesting to note that St. Augustine began to document the identity of its landladies and the location of its brothels only when it enacted its first ordinances outlawing prostitution in the late 1800s. Up until that time, prostitution and brothels were simply "business as usual" in the city and deemed invisible to polite society. Even after passage of laws making the businesses illegal, law enforcement took the stance that brothels were to be raided now and then to assure the public that the city was enforcing the laws, but as was true in the cases against Blanche Altavilla, very few convictions were sustained and no brothels were actually shut down. After all, the judges, the sheriffs and the men who constituted the juries were mostly longtime customers.

BOOZE! BOOZE! BOOZE!
He took a bottle up to bed
Drank whiskey straight all night
Drank Cocktails in the morning
But he never could get tight
He shivered in the evening
And he always had the blues
Until he took a bowl or two but he
never blamed the Booze.
His joints were full of rheumatics
His appetite was slack
He had pains between his shoulders
Chills chased up and down his back
He suffered from insomnia
At night he couldn't snooze
He blamed it on the climate
But he never blamed the Booze.
His constitution was rundown
At least that's what he said
His legs were swelled each morning
At night he had swelled head
He tackled beer, wine, whiskey
And if they ever failed to fuse
He blamed it on dyspepsia
But he never blamed the Booze.
He said he couldn't sleep at night

But always had bad dreams
He said he always laid awake
Till daylight's early beams
He thought it was malaria
But, alas! 'Twas but a ruse
He blamed it onto everything
But he never blamed the Booze.
His clothes was looking seedy
His beak was getting red
His children always hungry
Himself not too well fed
His family he neglected
His wife he did abuse
He blamed all of her relations
But he never blamed the Booze.
Next he had the jimjams
And he tackled bears and snakes
Next he had the fever
Then he had the shakes
At last he had a funeral
And the mourners had the blues
But he never blamed the Booze.
Think it over, and vote for
YOUR CHILDREN AND YOUR
NEIGHBOR'S CHILDREN
DRY! DRY! DRY!

—*front page,* St. Augustine Evening Record, *October 12, 1917*

4

A VERY THIRSTY TOWN

lcoholic beverages and the prodigious consumption thereof have always played a role in St. Augustine's history. As noted previously, a master brewer accompanied Pedro Menéndez on his trip across the Atlantic to found the colony for Spain. The new land proved advantageous for the growing of corn, sugar cane and other plants necessary for the fermentation process for hard spirits and for beer. Even better, muscadine (sometimes called scuppernong) grapes grew wild and made both a quite passable wine and, according to some opinions, a superior port. Production of alcoholic beverages required only that the distillation equipment be set up and a fire lit. Since the city also provided a fine harbor in Matanzas Bay, local importation of liquor, including fine wines and liqueurs from the Spanish homeland, Europe and the Caribbean began immediately as well. As soon as ships arrived in the new city, barrels of imported alcohol were rolling off onto the docks, ready for sale to the dehydrated population.

The first colonists quickly discovered that the water in the area was of poor quality, although plentiful. They had access to fresh water from artesian wells, which reeked of sulphur. This "rotten egg" water was the norm in St. Augustine until the 1960s and 1970s, when the city finally made treated water available citywide. This might account for the city's longtime reliance on alternative beverages to slake its thirst. To experience firsthand the drinking situation of the first colonists, go down to the Fountain of Youth, St. Augustine's first tourist attraction, which is located at the colony's original landing site, at 11 Magnolia Avenue in the north part of town. Drink from the fountain itself, one of the earliest artesian wells. The water may not make you younger, but the smell and taste will make you appreciate the skills of the local distilleries.

The speed with which taverns began to proliferate in St. Augustine, right on the heels of fortifications, housing for the colonists and a chapel, was also evidence of the new city's love for its fermented beverages. Citizens frowned on public drunkenness and the violent behavior that occasionally evolved out of overindulgence. Nevertheless, unless death occurred as a result, punishment was minimal. The authorities expected drunkenness, especially in a population primarily composed of soldiers, sailors and fishermen.

The manufacture of alcoholic beverages went unregulated. Most households produced such beverages for personal consumption, with any excess going for sale to other households or to taverns. The open market regulated alcohol sales—if you sold the good stuff, you prospered, but if your product was undrinkable, you sold cheaply or not at all. And so it went—until the Americans arrived.

During the centuries of Spanish and British rule, alcohol consumption in St. Augustine had been considered part of everyday living and certainly, in and of itself, was not classified as a wicked activity. Then the Americans came to town, bringing with them a Puritan heritage, a predominantly Protestant citizenry and, apparently, a close acquaintance with sin. By the 1820s, a temperance movement had sprung into existence. In 1832, the *Florida Herald* reported that "numerous and respectable" citizens of St. Augustine assembled at the Government House to form a new, official Temperance Society and establish a committee to "inquire into facts of intemperance and publish them to the world, as establishing an inquisition into our private affairs, which deserves the unqualified censure of this meeting." A deeper reading into the resolutions passed by the new Temperance Society reveals that the organization was in part formed because the respectable citizens had lost confidence in the older organization, which had "improperly demeaned itself" by "unjustly censuring a number of our best citizens." Politics, particularly where sin is concerned, never seems to change.

Around the time the United States acquired its new Florida territory, St. Augustine's population hovered somewhere around 1,500 souls, increasing in the next few years by about 1,000 as speculators and adventurers poured into Florida looking for excitement and ways to get rich quick. At one of its meetings, the local city council, while discussing the St. Augustine economy, noted that the annual consumption of "spiritous" liquors in the city was ten thousand gallons, or about six and a half gallons for every man, woman and child who lived there, and that the cost of this liquor to its consumers was equal to city profits from the production and sale of citrus. A light bulb, at this point, beamed brightly in the collective city council consciousness: the politicians realized that there was money to be had from taxing and licensing this previously unregulated activity (alcohol, not citrus) and so combined Puritan virtue and the regulation of sinful activity with all-American capitalism. The council didn't stop the manufacture or sale of alcohol, it simply charged for the privilege of doing so. This state of affairs remained constant until the early 1900s. With national Prohibition looming on the horizon, but not yet in effect, St. Augustine twice considered going dry.

At the time, the city was the wettest in all of St. Johns County. The county, except for St. Augustine itself, remained essentially dry, for the sole reason that it had no center of population large enough to support a tavern or a package store. This did not mean that no alcohol was produced or consumed in areas outside the city though. St. Johns County was a veritable paragon of alcohol production in the state of Florida. The southern part of the county was wine country. The abundance of local muscadine grapes in the Moultrie and Pellicer Creek areas ensured a regular flow of bottles to St. Augustine, where it could be consumed by locals and tourists alike. As for hard liquor, the corn and sugar cane fields of north and west St. Johns produced the ingredients necessary for "green shine," a highly volatile brew that, with

St. Johns County still seizure by Sheriff E.E. Boyce. Date unknown. *St. Augustine Historical Society.*

proper, skilled aging, could be transformed into a beverage that might even draw appreciation at the Ponce de Leon Hotel. The commercial production of beer, judging from court records, seems to have been a smaller industry, limited to home production in New Augustine and on Anastasia Island, but home-bottled beer still sold by the hundreds of cases in town. Going dry was a big decision for St. Augustine, considering the potential for hampering one of the largest factors in the local economy.

St. Augustine's drug business was less popular. In November 1902, *St. Augustine Evening Record* ran an article on its front page about Sam Wo's Chinese Laundry. The business, located at 22 Cathedral Street, the corner of Charlotte and Cathedral Streets, operated for a number of years as both a laundry and an opium den, catering primarily to the city's female population, who were forbidden by law to possess alcohol as an intoxicant. The article noted that the laundry had recently expanded to include booths for the purpose of accommodating opium smokers. The only complaint registered against the facility came from shopkeepers next door, who claimed that on occasion, strong, sickening odors emanated from the place. As far as can be determined by a review of the city newspapers and court records, no further community outcry ensued against Sam Wo, and the ladies of the city continued to use their opium, which was not an illegal substance at this time, as consolation for not being allowed alcohol.

On April 2, 1914, St. Augustine and St. Johns County held their first citizen referendum on going dry. At the time, the county was divided into eighteen election districts, and in all of the districts except for eleven and eighteen, the citizens voted to remain wet by a landslide. The county commissioners, as a way to take baby steps toward prohibition, decided that the vote did not mean that the entire county would remain wet. Instead, they decided that only those sections that voted to stay wet would remain so; districts eleven and eighteen, encompassing the city of Hastings, would now be dry. This being America, a lawsuit commenced immediately.

The Charles Blum Company, a corporation engaged in selling liquor, wine and beer and based in the town of Hastings, sued St. John's County and its five commissioners, alleging, among other things, improper and misleading ballots. Like the complaints around the 2000 presidential election ballots, the citizens said that a mark placed "For selling" could be interpreted as marked "Against selling." The lawsuit also alleged that properly registered voters were suddenly and inexplicably not permitted to cast their votes. They also argued the deprivation of their rights as citizens and, more importantly, taxpayers, since they had paid all their taxes and license fees in full for many

Site of the Cathedral Place opium den (Sam Wo's Chinese Laundry) as it appears today. *Author's collection.*

years. The new law, applicable only where the company was located, would create an undue burden on them, requiring them to move to another part of the county still wet.

The lawsuit was litigated in the circuit court for St. Johns County for over a year before it was dismissed in favor of the county and the county commissioners, with the Charles Blum Company to pay all the court costs. The final decree simply declared that "the equities [of this case] lie with the defendants." Hastings remained a tiny island of prohibition in a sea of liquor sales, and the Charles Blum Company moved.

In 1917, with World War I in full swing in Europe and millions of Americans actively serving in the conflict, temperance societies all over the country took the opportunity to step up their game. St. Augustine was no exception. The city hosted a number of well-attended temperance rallies, held both at indoor venues, mostly churches, and at open-air rallies on the plaza, attended by hundreds of citizens.

Their message was twofold: temperance for the sake of patriotism and temperance for the sake of the national economy. Love of one's country required that every community recognize its solemn duty to protect its youth by allowing children to grow up surrounded by good influences, good homes and good churches, all free of the evil influence of alcohol. As for the economy, the conversion of thousands of bushels of grain into alcohol took that grain out of the mouths of householders and wasted the country's natural resources. The temperance lecturers put the particular burden of working for prohibition of alcohol into the hands of the women of the community, as it was related to their duty to aid in the conservation of the national food supply through economy in the home. This was an interesting strategy, as in St. Augustine, as well as in other places throughout the United States, women were legally prohibited from either buying alcohol or casting a vote. It worked though, and on October 13, 1917, an ordinance, presided over by ladies at tea tables, passed in St. Johns County prohibiting the sale or consumption of alcoholic beverages. It passed by 45 votes, out of a total of 1,021 cast, with the newspapers attributing the 45 swing votes to the voters of New Augustine.

Even though the county was going dry, St. Johns and St. Augustine couldn't let go of their penchant for alcohol entirely. The new ordinance still permitted a householder to retain one quart of hard liquor per month and "a liberal quantity of beer," strictly for medicinal purposes and probably for the purpose of slaking one's thirst with something more palatable than the city water.

On September 29, 1917, prior to the referendum, local law enforcement called for the closure of all county taverns and liquor stores, allowing them time to get rid of all existing stock prior to it being declared illegal. The city went on a bender, attempting to assist the tavernkeepers and liquor salesmen in every way possible. Right after the referendum, on October 17, 1917, Stephens and Coe, the drugstore and pharmacy at 49 King Street, saw a merchandizing opportunity, advertising grape juice for sale at fifty cents a quart. In St. Augustine, you could still make wine for home consumption; Stephens and Coe were betting that the locals would do just that. They did—and much more.

In the three years between St. Johns County voting itself dry and nationwide Prohibition, many St. Augustine locals started and ran successful businesses running illegal liquor into the county and selling it. Avie Colee, Arthur Colee, James R. Colee, H.K. Jackson, Burton Masters, Harry Masters and Harry Canova were all cited for dealing in illegal liquor, with James R. Colee and Antonio Capo being cited for the additional unforgivable sin of selling alcohol to women and minors. In 1917, Mamie, Florence and

Lawrence Capallia and Elizabeth Bradfish were charged with transporting and selling wine in the city—sixteen barrels in the case of the Capallias. The year 1918 saw some additional interesting arrests: Paul Masters, for transporting illegal whiskey into the county and being intoxicated while doing it, and C.H. Canova, for bringing twelve gallons of whiskey into a dry county—while also acting as a law enforcement officer. The pattern of arrests with no convictions that seems to be prevalent throughout St. Augustine history still held, as the court records for all of these incidents contain no records of conviction for any of the offenses.

On January 17, 1920, after ratification of the Eighteenth Amendment by the requisite thirty-six states, all of America went completely dry, not even allowing the judicious use of alcoholic beverages for medicinal purposes. By then, St. Augustine's open manufacture of illegal liquor, beer and wine, as well as its flagrant consumption was in full swing. With taverns and package stores officially shut down, speakeasies and "private clubs," where payment of a membership fee entitled one to purchase and consume as much alcohol as one could afford, opened up all over town, even in the

Still seized by Sheriff E.E. Boyce (*center*) displayed in St. Augustine. Date unknown. *St. Augustine Historical Society.*

The Zorayda Club, 1907. *St. Augustine Historical Society.*

homes of some of its most reputable citizens. Some clubs, like the St. Augustine Yacht Club, the Bacchus Club and the Zorayda Club, catered to the very wealthy. The Zorayda Club in particular boasted a particularly well-stocked cellar. Its printed menu during Prohibition years, in addition to fine dining, contained an extensive list of imported wines that could be purchased, twelve different liqueurs, twenty-five different cocktails, twelve whiskies and assorted brands of gin, brandy, rum, ales, beers and ports. Other clubs openly selling alcohol, like the Charles F. Hamblen Club and the Tourist Club, served the lower income working men. Any man could get a drink in St. Augustine with very little effort; not much was changed from the wet days.

As for the manufacture and importation of illegal liquor, Prohibition brought a veritable renaissance to St. Augustine. Prior to Prohibition, making moonshine in large quantities was not a particularly profitable business. It requires an investment in land (moonshining generates significant, identifiable odors and requires considerable space to remain undetected by the discerning nose), equipment (cypress wood, iron and copper, all expensive and in short supply), grain (corn, barley and rye, with corn being the most common) and sugar. A bootlegger also needed a good supply of glass jugs, with five-gallon capacity being the most common, and an assortment of other bottles, including half pint, pint and quart, to accommodate the needs of individual customers. But by the start of Prohibition, the price of a single gallon of locally manufactured hard liquor in St. Augustine shot up to $60.00, which is equivalent to $256.09 in 2019 dollars. Operating a still became big business.

If you wanted the really good stuff and were willing and able to pay the large sums it commanded, you held out for the liquor brought into the city by its fleet of rumrunners. Since fishing had long been an occupation of residents, many of whom owned their own boats, a large number of local men became either part-time or full-time runners, picking up their cargoes of liquor in the Caribbean or in Cuba or by anchoring in international waters and waiting for liquor deliveries. The liquor then came into St. Augustine either through the inlet, with boats tying up and distributing bottles from docks lining the Avenida Menendez, or from the San Sebastián River, where cargo was unloaded at the shrimp docks on the east side of the river at the foot of King Street. David B. Green, a manager for the Florida

Still seizure, St. Johns County, 1954. *St. Augustine Historical Society.*

E.E. Boyce, mayor of St. Augustine, 1898–1906, and St. Johns County sheriff, 1917–1929. *St. Augustine Historical Society.*

East Coast Railroad living and working in St. Augustine during Prohibition, was interviewed in 1977 about his recollections of that time. One of his clearest memories was of a solid line of black cars nightly lining the south side of King Street, all waiting for low tide. The boats would come in to unload each night a total of one thousand to two thousand ham sacks of bonded whiskey brought in from the Caribbean.

The ham sack was invented for liquor smugglers. Each sack consisted of six bottles, wrapped tightly in straw and burlap and packed with salt. If the boat carrying ham sacks was boarded, the sacks were thrown overboard, where they quickly sank. By the time the boat had been inspected and the authorities were gone, the salt would have dissolved in the water, allowing the sacks and the liquor to float to the surface for easy recovery. Green recalled many of St. Augustine's most prominent residents patiently waiting in line at the San Sebastián dock for their ham sacks, including George Jackson, the local judge who issued all of the orders for illegal liquor seizures in St. Johns County during Prohibition, and E.E. Boyce, the sheriff of St. Johns County, who made all the moonshining arrests. He also recalled that speakeasies were on every street in the city and that all the men in town patronized them, from the highest to the lowest. Even the local ministers who preached temperance from the pulpit were, for the most part, to be found imbibing at the speakeasies in the evenings. As Green solemnly declared, "Observance of Prohibition [in St. Augustine] was very poor."

One of St. Augustine's most famous rumrunners was William McCoy, who was also the purported inventor of the ham sack. McCoy operated a boat taxi service for the Jacksonville–St. Augustine area and a boatyard where he built yachts for Andrew Carnegie, the Vanderbilts and others. When Prohibition hit, he recognized the opportunity for a new, more lucrative business enterprise. He sold the taxi service and the boatyard and bought a schooner, which he named *Tomoka*. McCoy would sail *Tomoka* (and later six additional vessels added to his fleet) to the Bahamas, fill it with the best rye, Irish, and Canadian whiskey he could purchase and then sail back to St. Augustine and anchor just outside the three-mile limit. The locals would then sail their own vessels out to the *Tomoka* and purchase what they needed, a perfectly legal transaction on McCoy's part. Bill McCoy became famous for the quality of his product and the fact that he never "cut," or diluted his liquor. When you bought from Bill, you were getting the "Real McCoy," and that is how we remember him today.

Unfortunately for McCoy, the Federal Revenue Service was not amused by his new business operation. On November 23, 1923, the U.S. Coast Guard cutter *Seneca* was ordered to capture McCoy and the *Tomoka*, even if it was operating in international waters and thus, outside the Coast Guard's legal jurisdiction. This is how McCoy described the incident:

> *When the* Tomoka *was boarded under the* Seneca's *guns, I immediately set sail and ran away with the boarding party—one lieutenant, one bosun and thirteen seamen—and only upon their pleas did I heave to and put them back on the* Seneca. *The damned radio was too severe a handicap for me. I surrendered after the* Seneca *had fired four-inch shells at me.*

The federal agents recovered 200 cases of whiskey out of a cargo of 4,200 cases, the other 4,000 cases having already been sold to McCoy's customers. After a lengthy trial, McCoy eventually pleaded guilty and served nine months in a New Jersey prison. Despite this, to his dying day he was proud that he never sold liquor in U.S. waters, never paid or accepted bribes from law enforcement and never, ever, worked with organized crime. He remained the Real McCoy.

Even though the most celebrated rumrunner was put out of commission in the early years of Prohibition, there were plenty of men to take his place. By 1926, rumrunning was commonplace off the St. Augustine coast, with the *St. Augustine Record* reporting that the Coast Guard was making regular forays into the city harbor looking (in vain, it is implied) for liquor smugglers. The article also pointed out that a walk on North Beach that day revealed 143 empty liquor cases for gin, rum, whiskey and champagne crowding a one-hundred-yard stretch of beach, the smugglers having "ham-sacked" all the bottles for delivery and then thrown the empty cases overboard. The reporter noted that there was a similar congestion of abandoned liquor cases for a stretch of over three miles on the St. Augustine coastline that day.

Citizens, in addition to being regular customers for smuggled liquor, did all that they could to keep their suppliers safe. Lookouts were posted along

Matanzas Bay. If the Coast Guard or revenue agents were in the vicinity and it was not safe, banners were suspended from the bridge between the mainland and Anastasia Island and lanterns lit in the upper stories and widows walks of the homes lining the bay front to alert the rumrunners.

Even though precautions were taken to ensure safe delivery of liquor, sometimes things went awry. One old-timer recalled a particularly momentous night when a schooner with a cargo of whiskey was attempting to negotiate the difficult currents of the inlet from the Atlantic into Matanzas Bay and somehow caught fire during the maneuvers. The ship and at least a portion of its cargo exploded, bringing out the entire population of the town to witness the spectacle. The citizens immediately mobilized to rescue the crew and what remained of the cargo, pulling them to safety on Anastasia Island. And then the town partied, consuming the evidence of wrongdoing in one glorious night.

Occasionally, despite the best efforts of the citizenry, the Coast Guard won. In August 1926, off the coast of Anastasia Island, the Coast Guard seized the schooner *Paloma*, known as the "Queen" of East Coast rumrunning. The *Paloma* was carrying over five thousand cases of choice liquor, estimated to be worth about $250,000.00 ($3,508,840.78 in 2019 dollars). The city deeply mourned its loss.

Local heroism and benevolent acts were often associated with illegal liquor transactions. The *St. Augustine Record* reported an incident in 1926 where a truckload of liquor collided with a bridge near the St. Johns County line, and in the words of the reporter, "the liquor ran like water." But thanks to the generous bootlegger and the concerned St. Johns County citizens, most of the liquor was saved and dispensed to the needy "for medical purposes."

Still, law enforcement made a nominal effort in the early days of Prohibition to comply with the terms of the Eighteenth Amendment. In May 1918, before national Prohibition was enacted but after St. Johns County had declared itself dry, Paul Masters, a prominent St. Augustine resident, along with four other men, was arrested and convicted of transporting illegal liquor into the dry county. His Ford Model T, used to transport the liquor, was seized by the county and forfeited as evidence. The convicted men were each fined between $500.00 and $200.00 ($8,479.87 to $3,391.95 in 2019 dollars). Although St. Augustine clearly intended to show that it was serious about staying sober, the business of illegal liquor was far too profitable to squelch totally. In fact, business increased. Paul Masters went on to be arrested numerous times for illegal transport and sale of bootleg liquor, the losses he incurred in arrest being far outweighed by the profits he made.

In 1920, Sheriff Boyce seized forty-seven quarts of Canadian Club whiskey from the Florida East Coast Railroad. Upon petition of the St. Johns County commissioners and the city commissioners of St. Augustine, the whiskey was "equitably distributed to the physicians of the Florida East Coast Hospital, Flagler Hospital and Worley Hospital" with the understanding that it be used to treat patients. The commissioners noted in their petition that they were making this decision based on the fact that "in the treatment of certain diseases and afflictions to which flesh is heir, it is the consensus of medical opinion that the use of whiskey is the most powerful aid known at the present time." Despite Prohibition, it was still the prevailing attitude in St. Augustine that to destroy good whiskey was a sin, especially when it could be put to charitable purposes.

New Augustine appeared to be a center for enforcement of the dry laws. On January 16, 1920, the day before Prohibition took effect, a thirty-gallon still, twenty gallons of mash and twenty gallons of moonshine were seized in New Augustine. The two moonshiners caught in the act were later acquitted after the sheriff deemed their product "not so palatable." To be arrested and convicted in St. Augustine, your shine had to at the very least be drinkable. In 1922 and 1923, Blanche Altavilla was arrested three times for possession and sale of intoxicating liquor, specifically dispensing said liquor from the two-gallon coffee urn in the main parlor of her Country Club brothel. Her still, which she operated nearby with her ex-husband, Sam, went untouched. In another twist, New Augustine vegetable peddler W.A. Roberts was severely beaten by four men, who accused him of "tipping off" the sheriff to the existence and location of their moonshining operation. The four men were arrested at a New Augustine lunch stand just over the San Sebastián Bridge, along with a "large quantity of shine," evidence of their guilt and the truth of Roberts's tips. They were convicted of the assault on Roberts—but not for producing or possessing moonshine.

Before the end of 1922, Sheriff Boyce announced publicly that henceforth he would conduct his war against local moonshiners on Sundays. Painting his new motto "The better the day, the better the deed" on the side of his Ford flivver, he declared that he would "don his shine-hunting uniform and sally forth" on each Sabbath day. To that end, he noted that on the prior Sunday he had "located and seized the largest still in captivity"—seventy-five-gallon capacity—along with four gallons of moonshine and three hundred pounds of sugar. Unfortunately, the operators of said still were never located.

This was the beginning of a cooperative system between law enforcement and moonshiners that kept St. Augustine swimming in illegal liquor and provided solid employment to St. Augustinians through Prohibition, through the Great Depression, through the World War II years and into the 1950s, until the manufacture of illegal liquor was no longer profitable. Boyce and his city counterpart, William Manucy Sr., the St. Augustine police chief, both recognized the value of the availability of alcoholic beverages and the right of a man to support his family by making them. They and their deputies had to walk a fine line between enforcing the law and adhering to their personal beliefs, so they invented a system that allowed for both. Federal revenue agents had to have proof that Prohibition was being enforced, so they usually accompanied the sheriff on raids. But deputies were sent out in advance to warn the moonshiners that a raid was scheduled, with the understanding that something had to be seized to pacify the federal agents and to show the good citizens of St. Augustine that Prohibition was being taken seriously. As law enforcement approached the chosen still, a bull horn announced their impending arrival and guns were fired into the air, giving the shiners who remained at the site one more chance to hide themselves.

Once the officers were on the scene, the distilling equipment was judiciously broken up into easily weldable pieces and taken into custody, along with whatever jugs of green shine (no one ever left the aged batches around for seizure) and fermenting mash remained. These items were usually carted off by the sheriff to the St. Augustine City Gates, where he posed for publicity pictures that would appear in the local newspapers or framed and hung on walls at the sheriff's offices, like trophies. Then the equipment was duly placed in custody at the sheriff's evidence locker until trial or, more usually, until the local shiner could be notified that his still was ready for pickup. After a little welding, full operation would resume within a day or two with little loss except for a few gallons of liquor, no doubt distributed to the needy for medical use.

Interestingly, in 1925, Florida governor John W. Martin wrote a letter to the St. Johns Board of County Commissioners. He had received numerous letters from the citizens of Hastings complaining about the activities of Constable Ralph Goodwin. (The position of constable being, at the time and up through the 1960s, an elected post, with the constable serving as a second to the county sheriff.) Constable Goodwin, in addition to his law enforcement duties, was apparently also conducting a lucrative business in wholesale dealing of liquor. Whether the citizens were concerned that his business was wholesale and not open to the public as opposed to retail

Moonshine seizure, St. Augustine, 1950. *St. Augustine Historical Society.*

and available to everyone or concerned that he was selling liquor at all is not known. We do know that Constable Goodwin did provide warning to shiners in advance of raids in the western part of St. Johns County and that he continued to do so for many years under Sheriff Boyce. Governor Martin's letter, which requested an inquiry into the constable's extracurricular activities, died a quiet death.

When Prohibition was in full swing and the cost of homemade liquor still high, a huge number of St. Augustine and St. Johns County residents became involved in the moonshine business, as it provided the steadiest source of employment and income next to working for Flagler's Florida East Coast Railroad. This new occupation sustained many a local family over the harsh years of the Depression and labeled St. Augustine as a place where a man could always find work and families would always eat. Making quality shine was not easy and required a degree of skill to properly prepare a mash for fermentation and to judge which results of the fermentation process would be drinkable and which contained so much methanol it could cause blindness or death if consumed. Aging techniques, which produced a higher quality, smoother-tasting shine that could bring significantly higher prices, varied among moonshiners. Some aged in white oak barrels and some added either charred fruit or local palmetto berries to their shine for color and taste. Certain shine producers became well known throughout the city for their excellent liquors, among them the Oesterreichers from Durbin Swamp, the Micklers from Palm Valley in northern St. Johns County and Streeter Canova, who operated his still at Lewis Point, just south of the city of St. Augustine. Known for the quantity of shine they produced but less so for the quality, was the Pacetti family,

Oesterreicher Place, Durbin Swamp, February 2003. Some of the best moonshine in the county was distilled here. Hugie Oesterreicher aged his shine in white oak barrels with charred peaches to give it a deep color and a smooth taste. *St. Augustine Historical Society.*

St. Johns County bootleggers' hunting party. *Right to left* (*top*): Lewis Dupont, Rufus Stratton; (*middle, standing*) Charley Stratton, Loring Hegman, Hugie Oesterreicher, Jesse Quigley, Willard Bennett (game warden), Isadore Stratton, Mr. Pacetti; (*bottom, sitting*) Sesemonde Oesterreicher, Marcus Pappy, Mrs. Fanny Bennett, Shelly Stratton, Mr. Juckett. Of the dogs in the image, two are identified as Ammus and Charlie, August 3, 1934. *St. Augustine Historical Society.*

whose stills lay in the tiny towns up and down State Road 16. This area of the county became known locally as "Pacettiville" and was the largest source of shine in the county.

The following snapshot based on seizures of stills and shine as detailed in the county court records for 1931 provides a good picture of how much illegal liquor was produced in St. Augustine and St. Johns County during Prohibition when production was at its height.

- Stills, mash and liquor were seized in the city of St. Augustine, New Augustine, Switzerland, St. Mark's Pond, Armstrong, Farrell's Still, Bakersville, Julington Creek, Moultrie, Twelve Mile Swamp, Cocoa Branch, Red Buck Branch, Pellicer Creek, Red House, Mill Creek, Turnbull Swamp, Casa Cola, Palm Valley, Fruit Cove, Elton, Deep Mouth Creek, Moses Creek, Rattlesnake Head, Six Mile Creek, Crescent Beach, Hurds,

Hardwood, Hastings, Oak Landing, Orangedale, Molasses Junction, Moccasin Branch and Matanzas. These locations constitute a comprehensive tour of St. Johns County.

- 48 stills were seized, with a combined capability of producing 119,490 gallons of shine per month.
- 22,020 gallons of mash, 2,531 gallons of moonshine, 225 gallons of wine and 5 gallons of beer were seized. The records also note that in this same year 1,402 bottles of homemade beer and 830 ham sacks (4,980 bottles) of bonded whiskey were also taken into custody.

These statistics clearly show that production of illegal liquor in the St. Augustine area during Prohibition was indeed substantial and confirms residents' accounts that literally millions of dollars of illegal liquor ran through the city, contributing massively to its economy at a time when the population of the entire county stood at ten thousand (eighteen thousand during the winter tourist season) and growing. Since the cooperative relationship between law enforcement and the local distillers was in full force and effect during this time, we can also conclude that the seizures reflect only the tip of the iceberg of actual production; many more stills operated than were actually seized. As for arrests and convictions of shiners, well, in the words of local lawmen, "The only ones who got arrested were the ones too drunk to run." No convictions for the operation of illegal stills were reported for 1931.

The locals and the tourists must have developed a taste for locally produced shine, because even after Prohibition ended and liquor could be produced, sold and consumed legally, the county and city moonshiners kept their operations running, albeit at a much smaller rate than they did during Prohibition. In addition, law enforcement tolerance was passed down from Sheriff Boyce to his successors, most prominently Sheriff L.O. Davis. Stills were raided and mash and liquor seized well into the 1950s, with a few arrests even extending into the early 1960s. One St. Augustine resident, Greg Carter, recalled accompanying his grandfather Noah Carter, then the St. Johns County constable, on Election Day visits delivering liquor to local judges, city officials and candidates up for election. When asked by his grandson why they were making the deliveries, Constable Carter responded that it was "just what law enforcement did on Election Day."

Moonshining was so popular it was even featured in a St. Augustine tourist attraction active in the 1950s called Moonshine Still. The attraction, located on State Road A1A, advertised itself as an "education exhibit, sanctioned by our state and federal governments" offering "the amazing sight of real moonshine stills in their natural wooded secluded site as captured in raids by revenue agents." The displays were of local stills, some seized by law enforcement and some voluntarily contributed by shiners who had gotten out of the business. Moonshine Still was not a success, however. It was too far off the beaten path for the tourists, and the locals already knew too much about the brewing of local shine. Everyone had a family member in the business, and everyone had a moonshine story to tell.

Distillation of spirits, now legal with the proper licenses, is still big business in St. Augustine. Top attractions include the St. Augustine Distillery on Riberia Street, City Gates Spirits on St. George Street, the San Sebastian Winery on King Street and numerous independent beer breweries scattered throughout the town. The art of moonshining, the unlicensed, illegal kind, flourishes as well. One well-known resident of West Augustine, who wished to remain anonymous, detailed his small-scale distilling operation, making "a real good bourbon," for consumption by friends, neighbors and relatives. He was very careful to stipulate that his liquor was never sold—only bartered. He also mentioned that every household he knew of in his neighborhood kept a five-gallon glass jug under the kitchen sink, where local fruit and green shine was turned into "special occasion brandy."

For quenching thirst (and to add to the reader's special recipes collection) nothing beats Prohibition Punch. The recipe appeared in the reminiscences of Roy Barnes, St. Augustine resident, who recalled making up batches of the punch for his parents' parties in 1936. It goes like this:

> *Grind up whole sour oranges, sweet oranges and grapefruits, enough to fill a porcelain bathtub. Pour 'em into the tub and add a good amount of sugar. Then fill up the tub with green shine. Don't ever use the aged stuff, it doesn't work as well. Let it all mellow for several days, then dip the whole mess into cloth sugar bags, squeeze it and strain it. What you get tastes like the mellowist whiskey sour you'll ever taste!*

After large-scale moonshining ceased in St. Augustine during the early 1960s, the drug trade took up the slack. Instead of ham sacks, law enforcement began picking up "square mullet" (marijuana bales) that floated in local waterways. Stills were replaced by methamphetamine labs. By 1973, the *St. Augustine Record* was running supplements to its editions warning the populace about the dangers of drugs and how to

Locals enjoying a little moonshine and music. Date unknown. *St. Augustine Historical Society.*

recognize the signs of usage and addiction, especially in the young. One such supplement, published on January 15, 1973, detailed the history of the "bad drugs," declaring that in the days prior to the 1950s and 1960s drugs had only been used to combat disease, but with the advent of "the pill" ("the first drug to be used to alter the body for our pleasure and convenience…causing women's lib, demise of the family and traditional marriage, and a breakdown of the dual standard"), drug use became rampant in society for personal pleasure. Today, a review of local arrests, published periodically in the *St. Augustine Record*, shows a multiplicity of drug possession, sale and production arrests. Rarely, if ever, do arrests involve prostitution, gambling or alcohol. And so history repeats itself… and wickedness endures.

5

MONEY TO BURN

*U*nlike the illegal production and sale of alcohol and the prostitution of women, the third in the trifecta of vices, gambling, was well established in the area that became St. Augustine long before the Spanish ever arrived on these shores. We have the account of Friar Juan de Paiva who described in detail the summer sports event of the Timucuans, native inhabitants of St. Augustine at the time the Spanish arrived. The game, called *el juego de pelota*, or the "ball game," was not only an annual celebration to entreat the deities for good crops but also the premier annual event for the Timucuans to indulge their favorite recreational activity—gambling. Friar Paiva reported that wagers on the outcome of the ball game were quite serious and could be as high as a family's entire possessions, including all of their food stored for the winter. He noted that so much was riding on the successful outcome of these games, villages would court the most skilled players by offering them free housing, free food and a free pass for their misdeeds from the local authorities. The Spanish immediately concluded that this game and all of its associated activities (which, among other things, included a temporary suspension of sexual prohibitions that existed between villages) were signs of the devil and a danger to the bodies (it was a violent game that could result in injuries and death) and souls of the natives. They therefore banned the game and all like it forever (at least until the NFL and college football came along).

While the Spanish may not have approved of the Timucuans gambling, they certainly allowed it as a recreational activity for their own colonists.

Timucuans playing el juego de pelota. Engraving by Theodor de Bry, 1591. *Florida Memory.*

Archaeological excavations of the first colony site turned up all manner of devices used for gambling, including bone dice, dominoes and pottery game markers. Early engravings depicting the colony show Spanish soldiers playing cards and casting dice. The taverns that sprang up all over the young city during the first Spanish period most certainly hosted gambling, in addition to food, drink and women as business draws. Activities introduced to St. Augustine by the Spanish that featured wagering included billiards, cockfighting, horse racing and card games. (Yes, billiard tables had already been invented. Billiards was first played in public in Italy in 1550, fifteen years before the founding of St. Augustine.) Early inventories of the wealthier denizens of the colony show gaming tables as common furniture items, indicating that taverns were not the only locations where gambling took place. Gambling activities have, through the centuries, remained a recreational mainstay in St. Augustine culture.

It is impossible to determine which of the gambling activities brought to St. Augustine by Menéndez's colonists took hold first. As noted, gambling on sports events began with the Timucuans, but all the rest appeared to have been popular from the get-go. Cards, dice, dominoes and other games loosely defined as "casino gambling" and involving both luck and skill were certainly established early and continued in popularity at least until the 1950s. The city didn't even get around to declaring gambling illegal until 1886, and even then casinos and open gambling abounded in many forms and many prominent locations.

The Ponce de Leon Hotel and the Alcazar Hotel both featured facilities dedicated to casino-type gambling, with the Ponce's gambling rooms, for gentlemen only, discreetly located downstairs from the dining area. The Alcazar's gambling areas were more openly established throughout the second floor of the hotel. Chicago brothers Edward R. and John "Jack" R. Bradley—both infamous gamblers but deemed gentlemen—opened the Bacchus Club at the corner of Cordova and Treasury Streets across from the Ponce in 1895. It was a private, invitation-only social club, accepting only the most affluent, distinguished and discreet into its membership. The club featured a first-class dining room on the ground floor and high-stakes poker games on the second floor. In 1895, the *Washington Post* wrote about the Bacchus Club, mentioning the huge amounts of money that exchanged hands on its second floor. One gentleman was able to fund his entire three-month winter season in St. Augustine, at $50.00 per day ($1,524.36 in 2019 currency), from his winnings at the Bacchus Club.

Shooting dice while waiting for the mash to cook. *St. Augustine Historical Society.*

Drawing of the Bacchus Club by H.S. Wyllie. *St. Augustine Historical Society Research Library Collection.*

The Zorayda Club, opened in 1903 directly across King Street from the Ponce de Leon, also contained first-rate dining facilities, open to the ladies for breakfast and lunch and to their husbands at night for dining, dancing and gambling. The Zorayda also featured one of the city's roulette wheels, in addition to poker, blackjack and other casino games of chance. The Zorayda even had its own celebrity high-stakes gambler, a gentleman who went by the sobriquet "Waco Kid" many years before the name was purloined for the movie *Blazing Saddles*.

The Lorillard Villa, on St. George Street between Hypolita and Cuna Streets where the Florida Cracker Café is today, was known as a gambling club for the wealthy and gained fame for its roulette wheel, one of the first in the city, and its poker tables. The St. Augustine Yacht Club was a long-established venue for discreet wagering, either on card games at its clubhouse on the St. Augustine bayfront or on the yacht races it regularly conducted during the winter season in the city.

For less well-heeled men, card games with lower stakes could be found at the Charles F. Hamblen Club or the Tourist Club. Substantial wagering also took place at card games at private residences throughout

The Lorillard Villa, on St. George Street, 1906. *St. Augustine Historical Society.*

the city. On January 17, 1919, and then again on April 7, 1919, raids were executed by Sheriff E.E. Boyce at homes throughout the city that resulted in the arrests of close to fifty individuals on each date for the crime of "gambling with cards." All but one of those arrested either had their cases dismissed or were acquitted by a jury of their peers. The exception was John Kennedy, who pleaded guilty to illegal card playing, although there is no record of his being assessed a fine or serving time for his crime. Once again, morality gave way to practicality and the desire to keep the local economy moving.

Later years show no diminution of St. Augustine's fascination with casino gambling. By the 1930s, over three hundred slot machines had been placed around the city, making gambling easy and accessible for even the most casual tourist. Just as popular as the slots, off-track betting parlors flourished, allowing bets to be placed on horse races all over the country from the comfort of downtown St. Augustine. The building at 124 Charlotte Street, which now houses the Tradewinds Lounge, was popular for its off-track betting, as well as for its card games and excellent liquor.

The St. Augustine Yacht Club as seen from the northeast corner of the Plaza, circa 1886. *St. Augustine Historical Society.*

The vast amount of money that was wagered in St. Augustine, especially during the tourist season, indicates that it wasn't only "honest" gambling that prospered, however.

Picture this scenario: an unsuspecting visitor to St. Augustine sits in one of the local gambling clubs, enjoying his bourbon, when he is approached by a well-dressed stranger who hospitably buys him a drink and engages him in friendly conversation about his stay in St. Augustine. The two men talk and drink into the evening, bonding over their mutual enjoyment of horse racing and reminiscing about their respective wins at betting tracks all up and down the Eastern Seaboard. Eventually, after a rapport has been established, the stranger tells the visitor that he just happens to work at one of the local off-track betting parlors, placing bets as an employee of a New York syndicate of gamblers. As with all off-track betting parlors in those days, bets would be placed before the races, and then the races would be called by announcers, reading the progress and results of races as they came off the ticker tape from the racetracks. The thing is, the stranger tells his new tourist friend, he has inside information from tipsters up north who

The Charles F. Hamblen Club (Blenmore), pre-1944. A hurricane that hit St. Augustine in that year destroyed the cupola topping the house. *St. Augustine Historical Society.*

Gambling Club located on Charlotte Street, now the location of the Tradewinds Lounge, 1920. *St. Augustine Historical Society.*

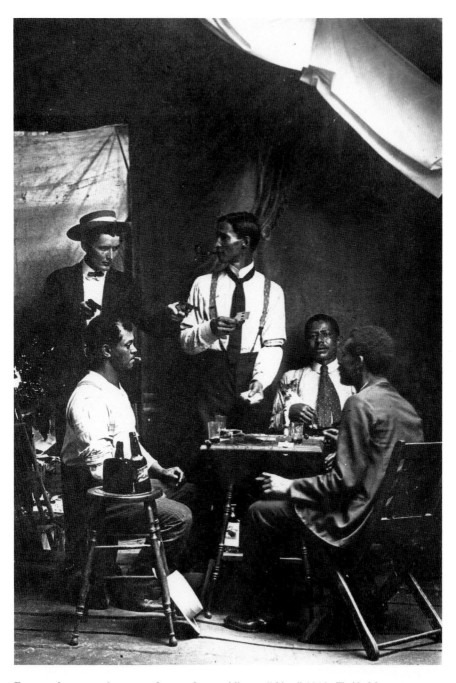

Four gentlemen on the verge of arrest for gambling at "skins," 1910. *Florida Memory.*

can get him race results via telegram and long-distance telephone before they ever hit the ticker tape. Pick the right race with the right odds and the two of them together can cash in big! The tourist sees this as a fabulous opportunity and agrees to meet his new friend at the Turf Exchange on the appointed day with his vacation funds, $20,000 in cash, to bet as directed by the northern tipster.

The Turf Exchange, located just outside the city limits, is a well-appointed club, equipped with black board charts, telephones and telegraphs, books, papers, betting tickets and stacks of money. It is bustling with business, men placing bets, announcers calling races, gentlemen lounging in comfortable chairs enjoying drinks between races—an altogether congenial place. Our visitor, a bit nervous about handling such a large amount of cash ($20,000 in those days equates to about $304,525 in 2019 dollars), looks about and spots his new friend at the bar.

"Place the bet on Sonny Boy in the third at Belmont," he whispers to the tourist, pointing to the open betting window as the "last call" is announced for bets on the third race. "My guy in New York confirmed it." The tourist jumps to the window and shoves over the pile of cash.

"$20,000 on Sonny Boy to win," he stammers.

"You sure?" says the man taking the bets. "That's a lot of money, pal. And this is the final bet."

The tourist hesitates slightly, but a nod and a smile from his friend at the bar steadies his nerves and he passes over the cash, receiving his ticket in return. The betting window closes. He then walks over to the bar to wait for the race results. The announcer, reading the ticker tape, begins to call the race. It is a close one, with the final result: Gallant Lad wins, with Sonny Boy placing second. Our tourist is horrified—he just lost his entire stake! Sonny Boy was supposed to win! His friend, equally agitated, accuses him of placing the wrong bet.

"I told you to put it on Sonny Boy to place, not to win! What were you thinking?" he shouts at the tourist.

Ashen and shaking at the immensity of his loss, the tourist grabs his companion by the lapels and begins to shove him, screaming, "You get my money back NOW!"

At this point, the hapless bettor is roughly picked up by two burly club bouncers and ejected. "Don't even think of coming back here," he is told. "Not ever."

Our tourist is left on the sidewalk, penniless, and choked with shame at having been swindled out of his fortune.

Does this scenario sound familiar? It reads like the script for *The Sting*, the Robert Redford and Paul Newman 1974 Oscar winner for Best Picture. But no. It is taken from the trial transcript in *The State of Florida vs. H.C. Mays, aka H.C. Sands* [the stranger], *C.H. Meyers, E.C. Collins, J. Eaton, Edward Phillips and George Clark*, a case that took place in St. Augustine in January 1919. The defendants ran the Turf Exchange as a front for "stinging" unwitting tourists out of their money.

It was only one of many such confidence games being run in St. Augustine during the first half of the twentieth century. The sidewalks of the city were full of tables where you could lose at Three-Card monte, the shell game, or bunco, as well as more elaborate scams, like the Turf Exchange. Unlike the gambling that took place at respectable clubs, law enforcement cracked down hard on those operations, small and large, designed specifically to scam the innocent tourist. The scammer hurt the economy and drove away the lucrative tourist business, which simply would not do. St. Augustine was never soft on crime when it was crime that alienated the tourist rather than attracting him.

Despite the occasional stain on horse race betting caused by enterprises like the short-lived Turf Exchange, horse racing and the gambling that went along with it remained a major business in St. Augustine, starting in the Flagler era. Flagler constructed a racetrack in the St. Augustine area, although to this day, its precise location remains a mystery. The *Florida Times-Union* did report on the racetrack's inaugural day: four hundred people attended, with multiple races filling out the day's card. Races also took place regularly on the city's hard-packed beaches, with local boys serving as jockeys and thousands of dollars wagered by the swells and their ladies who picnicked on the nearby sand dunes.

By the late 1940s, with parimutuel betting legalized in Florida, St. Augustine got really serious about horse racing. In 1946, the Florida Racing Commission granted St. Johns County a permit for a harness racing track, and the voters of the county passed a referendum to fund its construction. In February 1953, the million-dollar high-class Ponce de Leon Raceway, Florida's first nighttime harness track, was opened at the site of the old Keeney Park (once used in the 1920s for racing Thoroughbreds) in north St. Johns County, off of what is now Racetrack Road. Premium harness racing took place at the track annually during the tourist season until 1970, when harness racing was discontinued. The track was then renamed Gator Downs and used for racing quarter horses. In 1974, horse racing ended altogether. The track was refitted for greyhound racing and renamed the St. Johns

The Ponce de Leon Raceway, 1954. *St. Augustine Historical Society.*

Greyhound Park. The greyhound track, which included poker tables in the clubhouse, operated successfully until 2000, when the track was shuttered for good and racing moved to Jacksonville. Wagering on live races is now a memory in St. Augustine but a hallowed one.

Cockfighting, another longtime animal-based gambling activity, has been highly popular in Florida since the Spanish first set foot on its shores. St. Augustine was no exception. There are no documents indicating when it first started in the city, but it was probably at the same time the city acquired its first roosters, during the days of the first colony. The sport, and the wagering that accompanied it, was at its height in the state for the hundred-year period from 1840 to 1940, when cockfighting was not only legal but also cultish in its formality and ritual. Cockfights were held regularly in arenas constructed especially for its spectacle.

In St. Augustine, there were many small, informal venues for fighting, at least two of which were built in Flagler's heyday for use by the high rollers. The Alhambra Hotel on Granada Street (also known in its earlier days as the Granada Hotel) had areas within the hotel fitted out for cockfights. The St. Augustine Game Club built a special facility for cockfighting just outside of town adjacent to the municipal airport on what is now Gun Club

Road. A big-time operation, on several occasions the Game Club hosted the International Cock Fighting Tournament. The finest fighting birds in North America and, indeed, from all over the world, competed for loving cups and thousands of dollars in prize money. Hundreds of thousands of dollars were wagered on the success of the top birds.

Betting was an essential feature of cockfighting. Old-timers in St. Augustine recall that while the standard bet minimum at a contest was around $100, bets of $1,000 to $10,000 per contest were not unusual. During a four-day individual meet, over three hundred birds would compete, with huge sums of money won and lost, all without a single dollar being flashed or a word spoken. Bets were made by hand gesture or head nods, with amounts jotted on the backs of envelopes. The contests themselves were pretty straightforward: a rooster won when his opponent became too weak to continue or died during the fight. Bettors either lost their shirts or triumphed to the tune of thousands of dollars. Trainers and handlers of good fighters could plan on taking home a minimum of $1,500 per day in fees and hedged bets on their birds. As for the valuable roosters, some of whom would be flown into meets by private airplanes, very few lasted more than two or three fights. After that, they ended up in kitchen pots.

Although cockfighting in St. Augustine seemed to be an open sport, publicly advertised and widely attended, a certain secrecy had to be maintained. Cockfighting was a legal sport in Florida until 1976, when the first state statute was passed banning the sport as cruelty to animals. What *was* illegal at all times was the wagering that accompanied the sport. That is why bets were placed silently, leaving no interpretable written record of wagers—just in case local law enforcement or a federal agent might be in the crowd.

Not surprisingly, the same spirit of cooperation that existed between law enforcement and good men trying to make a living dealing in the vices of alcohol and women was just as strong for gambling. In fact, there are even fewer references in the city records for infractions of the law related to cockfighting than there are for any of the other vices. The only mention of a major arrest appeared in the March 20, 1966 edition of the *St. Augustine Record*. It recounted a raid at the St. Augustine Game Club arena on Gun Club Road during the regular Friday afternoon cockfights. The raid caught the attendees by surprise. According to Constable Noah Carter's account to his grandson Greg Carter, the raid had local businessmen, judges and lawmen, as well as a newspaper reporter or two, jumping out of the facility windows and scampering into the nearby woods. Only a few of the two hundred–plus attendees were actually caught and charged, with all but one released on bond. Constable Carter estimated that over $500,000 ($3,950,204.40 in 2019 dollars) were in play as bets during this tournament, with $1,000 being the average bet, based upon the testimony of undercover agents who had been present. At the scene, $11,000 cash was left behind by panicked gamblers and confiscated by law enforcement, along with gambling paraphernalia, cockfighting equipment and a number of lucky roosters. The St. Augustine Game Club collected admission tickets for the event: $8.00 to attend the competition plus $0.18 "tax" for each ticket, revenue that most certainly was never remitted to the state revenue office.

Cockfighting, even though now illegal, still continues in Florida and probably in St. Augustine, although the Alhambra Hotel is long gone and the cockfighting arena on Gun Club Road is ostensibly closed, though still in existence. Aficionados of the sport, most notably the Association for the Preservation of Gamefowl, have sought to re-legalize it and to protect the rights of citizens engaging in cockfighting, looking to the 1821 treaty between Spain and the United States establishing Florida as a U.S. territory as a source for those rights. As for legalizing the gambling that inevitably accompanies cockfighting, don't start counting your roosters just yet.

The last gambling sport is also the one most tinged with respectability: billiards. Notwithstanding Professor Harold Hill's admonition that "trouble, with a capital T, and that rhymes with P and that stands for pool" in *The Music Man*, St. Augustine embraced billiards early on. Billiard tables appear in city records as early as 1702, with the earliest permit for a commercial billiard table being issued to Joseph Pomar in 1821. By the time of Florida's admission into the union as a state in 1845, numerous such commercial licenses had been issued in the city. By 1851, billiard tables were already being used as incentives to tourists visiting the city, with hotels boasting in their advertisements of "gentlemen-only billiard rooms, open through the day and evening" for their entertainment. Henry Flagler wholeheartedly embraced billiards for his hotels, obtaining licenses for six pool tables in the Ponce de Leon Hotel and three pool tables in the Alcazar Hotel in 1894. Advertisements for the hotels as well as newspaper accounts of the luxuries provided at the hotels prominently featured the presence of the billiard tables, declaring the sport to be "the favorite amusement" of St. Augustine.

Dr. Andrew Anderson, owner of the Markland estate adjoining the Ponce de Leon Hotel and close confidant of Henry Flagler, made his private "Billiard House" on the estate available for recreation and wagering to a select group of wealthy seasonal visitors. Meanwhile, billiard parlors and pool halls (same thing essentially, with the terminology dependent on their attendees' social status) were springing up all over the city, for the use of locals and tourists alike. Blanche Altavilla installed pool tables at her Country Club in New Augustine. The Charles F. Hamblen Club for the working men of St. Augustine boasted of its pool tables, declaring, "Not all the men could play real good, but they'd wait for hours just to play one game." By the late 1940s, the number of licenses for pool tables in the city declined sharply, but that didn't mean the number of actual pool tables located in commercial spaces decreased. A check of licenses issued for the decades from 1950 to 2000 shows few licenses issued and in some years none at all. But pool halls persist, as do pool tables as regular fixtures of taverns and sports bars throughout the city. Unlike cockfighting, playing pool remains a legal means of entertainment—just don't place any wagers on the game. Betting will bring trouble with a capital T.

GOOD TIMES INDEED– ST. AUGUSTINE'S ENTERTAINMENT SECTORS

The City

The Dewdrager's Ditty

Hear that music playing,
Makes you feel like swaying,
Here those folks all saying,
We are headed for that big Dewdrager Ball,
Come and join our party, put your troubles away,
You'll get a welcome hearty,
We'll show you how to play.
Cause I mean, when you hear,
A sound of jazzy dancin',
Joyful feet a'prancin',
Voices raised in musical song,
Boys and Sweeties struttin' along,
Then you'll know,
We are goldenrod glad to be alive and kickin',
Come and let's make it snappy,
Hot Dog—Everybody's feelin' happy,
Keep that pep up at the old Dewdrager's Ball.
DANCE 'TILL YOU FALL.

*W*hen Henry Flagler began his odyssey remaking St. Augustine in 1883, he may not have anticipated the effect his development would have on the city's demimonde. During the Gilded Age of the late 1800s to the early 1900s, in the Roaring Twenties and particularly during Prohibition, the gentility promoted by Flagler was merely a veneer supported by an underworld of illegal entertainment designed for gentlemen of money and position. The city can be compared to New Orleans's famous Storyville district, only less publicized. Men with money to spend availed themselves of the services of women, increased or diminished their fortunes through high-stakes gambling and enjoyed an abundance of both illegal and legal liquor—even on Sundays and after passage of "dry" ordinances made the sale of such beverages prohibited by law. Flagler and his political cronies tacitly approved these activities in St. Augustine and St. Johns County, as did the local politicians. The movers and shakers who followed Flagler turned a blind eye except when it became politically expedient to have an arrest or two (or three) to satisfy public morals.

The areas where the more adult-oriented entertainments could be had can be pinpointed within the city parameters. Charlotte Street was known for centuries in St. Augustine as a location for brothels and prostitution as well as a center for legitimate commerce. At least two, and possibly three brothels mentioned in the city records were located on Charlotte Street north of King Street, with another located on South Charlotte Street at the northeast corner of Charlotte and Cadiz (now a vacant lot). A photograph of the South Charlotte Street brothel and its gardens taken before its demolition is labeled as "The Old Cat House"—and the writer definitely did not mean the location was used for the breeding of felines.

Testimony in a number of criminal trials stated that primarily women of color conducted business on Charlotte Street, both in the brothels and individually, and that this had not changed in St. Augustine's history. Early maps of the city show a concentration of homes and boardinghouses in this area owned and rented by single women of color and listed both as domiciles and unspecified "businesses." Ocie Martin, the preeminent black landlady in Lincolnville, probably owned and operated one of the Charlotte Street brothels. Although there are no city records that show such ownership, there are civil court records mentioning Martin housing young ladies in her employ in "one of her houses" on Charlotte Street.

Ocie Martin's house in Lincolnville on Bridge Street advertised itself as a restaurant and music venue. The house at 80 Bridge Street, just a

"The Old Cat House." Photo of abandoned house on the corner of Charlotte Street and Cadiz, taken at the turn of the twentieth century. *St. Augustine Historical Society.*

stone's throw from Trinity Methodist Church and less than a block from Lincolnville's popular Washington Street nightclubs, was renowned as a center for entertainment both because of the beauty and sophistication of the women who worked there and for the quality of its offered diversions. In taped interviews many years later, Ocie's patrons disclosed that from that facility she also provided the prettiest, most refined girls in town, all imported from New York City and of mixed race.

Although racial integration had been the norm in the city since the first Spanish period, Henry Flagler insisted upon strict segregation on behalf of his white northern guests, who were quite uncomfortable with contact with other races except as servants. There were, however, no racial boundaries applicable to wealthy males seeking female companionship for a limited time. Ocie was the landlady to call if you wanted a well-dressed, healthy, attractive woman of color.

Ocie Martin did not limit her trade to the wealthy. She also operated another house just outside of the northern city limits that catered to working men, both black and white, and probably obtained much of its custom from

Flagler's railroad employees. In addition to these two houses, Martin also owned a house at 80 Park Place in Lincolnville, which was both her personal residence and, by some accounts, a brothel as well. That house, which is now a private residence, appears in the photographs of Ocie Martin taken by prominent Lincolnville photographer Richard Twine in the 1920s.

Margaret Jones (aka Margaret Darling) operated another upper-end brothel in Lincolnville at 39 Sanford Street. The house was listed in St. Augustine records as a "boardinghouse," often a euphemism for a brothel. Mrs. Darling was arrested numerous times, sometimes in tandem with her husband, Jack, who owned the house across the street at number 38. Today, these houses are lovely upscale private residences, belying their once wicked past.

In a curious bit of history, Blanche Altavilla, the most prominent landlady during this period, acquired part of the land on which her Country Club was located in New Augustine from Margaret Darling. Margaret, in turn, appears to have operated a brothel predating the Sanford Street operation on what later became the Country Club property under Blanche's ownership.

Ocie Martin's house today. *Author's collection.*

Margaret Darling's house at 39 Sanford Street, as it appears today. *Author's collection.*

Blanche also owned a large house in this part of town, located at 113 La Quinta Place, next to the stables owned by the Colee family's St. Augustine Transfer Company. Mayme Colee, Blanche's ex-husband's new wife, sold her the house. There are no records in St. Augustine indicating that Blanche operated a brothel or any other illegal operation out of the house on La Quinta Place, but then Blanche was never one to let fertile ground lie fallow. Blanche's former house is also now a private residence.

On King Street sat Flagler's three showcase properties: the Alcazar Hotel, the Cordova Hotel (now the Casa Monica) and the Ponce de Leon Hotel. While the three hotels could by no means be characterized as brothels, they were, as mentioned before, locations where assignations with St. Augustine's ladies-for-hire were arranged and consummated with great regularity.

Assignations at the Alcazar Hotel occurred on the fourth floor, in that section of the hotel reserved for bachelors. The rooms, which still exist and can be toured, are small and simply but elegantly furnished. When a guest sought non-spousal companionship in addition to or even instead of a carnal

Jack Darling's house, 40 Sanford Street, as it appears today. *Author's collection.*

encounter, the Alcazar provided the opportunity for dining, dancing and gambling two floors below. The Grill, located in the northeast corner of the Alcazar, was a popular nightclub where swells and their dates could spend the evening dining, dancing, drinking and indulging in games of chance. St. Augustine old-timers say that the ladies provided to the Flagler hotels by the

House on La Quinta Place owned by Blanche Altavilla. *Author's collection.*

more well-regarded landladies were indeed of a caliber that could be taken into the public eye without fear of embarrassment or censure. They were always elegantly and properly dressed and with impeccable manners.

Unlike the Alcazar, where recollection of both employees and patrons confirm where and how prostitution and other vices were conducted, there is no such confirmation for the Ponce de Leon and Cordova Hotels, although they most certainly provided the services in some form or another. On-site gambling, however, was another animal entirely.

The wealthy and powerful winter visitors to the Ponce de Leon could take their ease after the elaborate meals in the Ponce's elegant dining room, with its windows by Louis Comfort Tiffany, in the men-only bar and gaming rooms located discreetly downstairs and underneath the dining area. If the gentleman was a particular friend of either Flagler or Dr. Andrew Anderson, Flagler's closest St. Augustine associate and owner of Markland (the sumptuous plantation mansion next door to the Ponce de Leon Hotel), he might be invited to the tiny Billiard House. This venue, built by Dr. Anderson between 1899 and 1901 and now known as Markland cottage,

The Alcazar Hotel, as it appears today. *Author's collection.*

The Casa Monica Hotel, formerly the Cordova Hotel, as it appears today. *Author's collection.*

Bachelor's quarters on the fourth floor, Alcazar Hotel. *Author's collection.*

sits at the rear of the Markland property. It provided an intimate space for the masculine pastime of billiards and the wagering that accompanied the games, and Dr. Anderson spared no luxury. The cottage has been restored to its 1901 appearance, complete with marble bathroom, Majolica-tiled fireplace and imported sycamore wainscoting, doors, columns and trim. The renovation preserved one telling souvenir of good times at the billiards table. In the center of the meticulously restored vintage pine tongue-and-groove flooring, the cigar burns have been left intact.

The Ponce de Leon and its super-wealthy patrons also utilized The Bacchus Club, an invitation-only gentlemen's dining facility located across from the Ponce de Leon's carriageway at the northeast corner of Cordova and Treasury Streets. Opened in 1895 by Edward and John Bradley, originally from Chicago, the lower floor was operated as a world-class dining facility for invited (which means wealthy) men. Local advertisements for the Bacchus Club touted its "first class chefs, cuisine and service, with breakfast, lunch and dinner offered at all hours. Private parlors are offered for parties of any number at any hour." Upstairs, the Bradleys ran a discreet,

The Billiard House on the Markland estate, restored to its original appearance. *Author's collection.*

high-stakes gambling operation for the entertainment of club patrons. The entertainment at the Bacchus Club likely also extended to the arrangement of short-term female companionship for the patrons. Surely the gentlemen availing themselves of the private parlors offered at all hours could not be expected to dine exclusively in the company of other wealthy men. Unfortunately, there is no hard proof of what activities were included at the Bacchus Club other than dining and gambling.

In addition to the three Flagler hotels, a later addition to this premium hotel district also provided a posh though more reasonably priced accommodation for assignations with St. Augustine's ladies for hire. Located at the corner of King and Granada Streets, across from the Alcazar front gardens, the Alhambra Hotel, earlier called the Hotel Granada, and the Zorayda Club, now called the Villa Zorayda, were owned by the same family, the Mussalems. The two facilities operated in happy tandem, hosting fine dining, premium spirits and high-end gambling at the Zorayda and providing venues for illicit rendezvous and cockfighting, another popular gambling activity, at the Alhambra. The Alhambra was lost to fire in the

Site of the Bacchus Club, northeast corner of Cordova Street and Treasury Street, as it appears today. *Author's collection.*

1950s, but the Mussalem family still owns the Villa Zorayda, a popular tourist attraction on King Street, where menus, liquor lists, playing cards and a roulette wheel from the "good old days" are now on display.

During its history, St. Augustine has hosted a number of United States presidents, including Ulysses S. Grant, William McKinley, both Theodore and Franklin Roosevelt and Lyndon Johnson. Most of them stayed at the Ponce de Leon Hotel. However, the city's most celebrated presidential visitor to the Ponce de Leon Hotel during the Gilded Age was Warren G. Harding.

Harding vacationed at the Ponce de Leon numerous times, both as a private citizen and after he became the twenty-ninth president of the United States. The hotel became a virtual winter White House for Harding, who is said to have conducted much presidential business there, including selecting his cabinet. It was even rumored about town that the position of postmaster general was decided by a golf game played at Harding's favorite local links.

Harding was much beloved in St. Augustine and was feted with dinners, concerts, public ceremonial events and society balls every time he visited, either formally or informally. He moored his yacht at A.J. Corbett's dock

(Remember A.J. Corbett? He was Blanche Altavilla's attorney, and his dock also contained the St. Augustine Yacht Club clubhouse) on the bay waterfront just south of the Plaza. Harding played golf at the local St. Augustine Links, often thirty-six holes a day. He liked to stroll St. George Street in the early morning hours and often went to movies at the theaters on Cathedral Place, stopping to mingle and socialize with the locals.

A noted womanizer, his assignations with women other than his wife, Florence, were not just confined to the White House. In fact, his affinity for St. Augustine was probably not limited to the weather, his comfortable suite at the Ponce de Leon or his favorite golf course. Harding, a personal guest of Henry Flagler, would have likely considered it only proper to patronize not only the establishment of fellow Ohioan Blanche Altavilla but also to sample the other local delights available to Flagler's wealthy male clients, including the fine food and entertainment offered by the local gambling clubs, especially the St. Augustine Yacht Club and the Zorayda Club.

When President Harding expired the evening of August 2, 1923, the headlines the next day announcing his death stunned St. Augustine. The

Hotel Granada, later known as the Alhambra Hotel, shown from King Street. Date unknown. Note the Alcazar Hotel next to it, across Granada Street. *St. Augustine Historical Society.*

The Villa Zorayda as it appears today. *Author's collection.*

entire city went into deep mourning: banks and theaters were closed, memorial services were held for the public in the plaza and all trains on Flagler's Florida East Coast Railway were ordered to stop for five minutes in Harding's memory. The city also sent a delegation to Harding's funeral in Marion, Ohio, where they were served luncheon with the First Lady, Florence Harding, at the home where Harding's body was lying in state. Later, they placed a floral representation of the City Gate at the Harding vault in the Marion cemetery. After Harding's passing, St. Augustine's wicked industries never again hosted a patron of such national political prestige.

During the Gilded Age, the Roaring Twenties and even in years up to and including World War II, gambling was certainly close to the top of the list as the preferred recreation for men, both those visiting and those residing in St. Augustine. Only steps away from the Flagler hotels was the Villa Zorayda, also known during different times as the Zorayda Club, the Zorayda Castle and Zorayda House. It was built in 1883 by the Boston millionaire Franklin W. Smith for use as his summer home but in 1903 became a center for evening entertainment as a nightclub and gambling casino. On the other side of King Street, the building that is now the Tradewinds Tropical

President Warren G. Harding on vacation in St. Augustine in 1921. *St. Augustine Historical Society.*

Tradewinds Lounge as it appears today. *Author's collection.*

Lounge and Grill, located at 124 Charlotte Street, was another popular spot for high-stakes gambling, off-track betting and slot machines.

Crossing to the sector of St. Augustine north of King Street, the number of known brothels drops dramatically, and verification of those sites is mostly by word-of-mouth and rumor. During the Gilded Age, this part of town was Flagler's domain and included his "Model Land" neighborhood, where he built homes, both elaborate and modest, to house his friends, business associates and employees. Efforts were made to keep the reputation of this area as wholesome and family-friendly as Flagler wanted it to be. The Bacchus Club, discussed previously, was a clear exception, although use of its entertainments was confined to specific wealthy white males.

The Lorillard Villa, located on the east side of St. George Street north of Hypolita Street, south of Cuna Street and taking up most of the block where the Florida Cracker Café now stands, was a popular gambling club for much of its existence. Known to the locals as "Gilbert's Gambling Den," the Lorillard Villa boasted a roulette wheel and poker tables and was among those clubs in town that catered to the wealthy northern visitor and habitué of the finer hotels. Well-regarded for the safety of its operation, the Villa had an arrangement with local law enforcement to receive advance notice of any impending raids. Because of this system, men who chose the Lorillard Villa to indulge their gambling habit were rarely caught, which would account for the dearth of gambling charges against individuals coming from this location. The Villa itself was cited on several occasions as an illegal gambling house (for which fines were levied and paid quickly) but was never shut down and was never cited as a house of ill fame, even though the two charges often went hand-in-hand.

Several brothels allegedly operated on Spanish Street, calling themselves "female boardinghouses," one near the City Gates and one farther south. An oral history provider, though not mentioning the specific address, wondered why a particular home on Sevilla Street, deep in the heart of Flagler's Model Land, had been broken into numerous tiny bedrooms, each barely big enough to fit a twin bed and a nightstand. Since that is a typical brothel floor plan, allowing for maximum utilization of space for services to be rendered, chances are Sevilla Street also housed working girls supervised by a St. Augustine landlady, although her name is lost to history.

The Parks Hotel at 24–22 St. George Street is often mentioned by old-timers as a location preferred by prostitutes for their temporary assignations. The hotel was operational from the mid-1920s until the mid-1960s. According to the residential neighbors on St. George Street, the Parks was the scene of much revelry and shady activity, hosting a revolving door of working girls and their clientele. Their noisy festivities, extending most nights into the early morning hours, kept the local schoolchildren up way too late, but also boosted their curiosity and powers of observation to astounding levels.

In the early centuries of St. Augustine's existence, most of its wicked activities were concentrated on the bay front, that portion of town that bordered Matanzas Bay and faced the inlet that allowed ships ingress and egress to the Atlantic Ocean. Here sailors, soldiers and fishermen congregated and taverns proliferated. Cases of rum, gin, brandy, whiskey and wine, brought in from Cuba and the West Indies, were unloaded at the docks and stockpiled for future sale in the warehouses that lined the bay. The usual vices mushroomed as the city's wealth and population expanded. By the time of the tourist boom instigated by Henry Flagler, the city had declined as a seaport and center for trade, and its shipping wharves and warehouses had all but disappeared. Their space on the bay front was replaced by the new top industry, hotels that catered to tourists with money

Site of the former Parks Hotel on St. George Street as it appears today. *Author's collection.*

The Parks Hotel, date unknown. *St. Augustine Historical Society.*

to spend and other businesses ensuring great quantities of that money went into the local economy.

In the early part of the twentieth century, Hotel Bennett was built on the waterfront at the northwest corner of the intersection of Charlotte and Cuna Streets. The hotel touted in its advertisements that it was "modern, new and up to date." It featured steam-heated rooms (some with private baths), electric elevators and "private sunny piazzas overlooking the bay and ocean." Best of all, it was moderately priced. You didn't need the income or breeding of a Rockefeller to book a room for the season at Hotel Bennett.

This worked out well for the local working girls, who booked rooms at its reasonable rates and utilized its comfortable restaurant and lounge for the entertainment of customers. Apparently, Hotel Bennett was a step up from the nearby Parks Hotel, since the ladies hosted a more genteel clientele. Arrest records and neighborhood recollections suggest far fewer parties and disruptions of the peace occurred at the Bennett than at the Parks. Maybe it was the peacefulness acquired from lounging on those sunny private piazzas facing the bay.

Farther south along the bay, on a pier across the street from the plaza, close to today's approach to the Bridge of Lions, stood the headquarters of the St. Augustine Yacht Club. After the Civil War ended, St. Augustine began its career as the winter playground of northern industrialists. Those prestigious families—Rockefellers, Colgates, Stuyvesants, Flaglers and Vanderbilts among them—flocked to the city's warm, orange blossom–scented shores. They brought their private yachts with them. The protected bay and the Matanzas River, with easy Atlantic Ocean access, provided the perfect place to engage in the pastime of yacht racing, especially since it was only blocks away from their winter residences at the best hotels.

The St. Augustine Yacht Club was officially founded in 1873 and officered by a commodore, a vice-commodore and a secretary-treasurer. The club established a regatta committee to arrange social events, races and competitions. The official season was limited to four months out of the year, beginning January 1 and ending on May 1. Official nautical uniforms were designed and mandated for all members of the club.

The first clubhouse was at the Dowling Dock on Water Street, just north of the Castillo, but was later moved in the late 1800s to the city wharf at

The Bennett Hotel, 1958. *St. Augustine Historical Society.*

the foot of Cathedral Place, opposite the plaza. This space, a two-story, gable-roofed structure, was described by the *Florida Times-Union* as "richly furnished and elegantly decorated." The *Tatler*, a local society publication, described it as "affording a beautiful view of the city, bay and ocean; its veranda a delightful lounging-place; the rooms simply furnished, cool, mattings, bamboo furniture, card tables where wonderful games of whist are conducted, shelves filled with magazines, newspapers and books, making it extremely attractive." The *Tatler* later praised the yacht club for offering its members "food for the mind and amusements of a quiet order," which included card-playing and cigar smoking. By 1892, at the height of the popularity of the Flagler hotels, the membership of the yacht club had grown to eighty, and the seasonal regattas, races and society balls hosted by the club were legendary.

Although not described in the official annals of the yacht club, the club's reputation as the place where the rich went to gamble has been documented in the oral histories of locals. Literally millions of dollars were wagered on those quiet card games, games of chance and, of course, yacht races.

The interest in yacht racing diminished in the early 1920s as steam yachts became more popular modes of transportation for the wealthy. Gambling at the St. Augustine Yacht Club, however, continued, and the club prospered to the point that construction on a new luxury facility in Davis Shores, across the bay on Anastasia Island, began. But the Depression of the 1930s brought an end to the new club headquarters, which was never finished, and to the yacht club itself, which was decommissioned in 1939, after a fire in January of that year damaged the old club beyond repair. The St. Augustine Yacht Club had lasted sixty-seven years. (Note: The yacht club was recommissioned in the late 1970s and continues in operation today as Florida's Oldest Yacht Club. It is headquartered on the Salt Run on Anastasia Island, caters to the not-as-wealthy-as-Rockefellers and is no longer known for its high-stakes gambling. Not that we know of.)

While St. Augustine had a clear fixation with the very wealthy (that's where the money is), those of low to moderate income also had ample opportunities for losing that income through organized gambling. Directly across the street from the St. Augustine Yacht Club and facing the plaza on Anderson Circle at the intersection of Cathedral Place and Avenida Menendez is the Hamblen House. Charles F. Hamblen arrived in St. Augustine with his wife, Antonia, in 1874, from Stillwater, Maine. Hamblen was a successful entrepreneur and built one of the longest-lived businesses in the city, Hamblen Hardware, located on King Street. He and his wife built the two-and-a-half-story building on the bay as their home and named it Blenmore.

Known for his business achievements, Hamblen was a pillar of St. Augustine society, and Blenmore hosted a number of gala social gatherings. Hamblen was also a man who remembered his community. The *St. Augustine Record* described him as "unfailingly helpful and charitable when appeals were made to him for aid, and many individuals and organizations throughout the city have reason to appreciate his kindliness and generosity of spirit." This affinity for the common man was made even more apparent when Hamblen's will was read after his death at the age of eighty-four on December 29, 1920. Hamblen (whose wife predeceased him) left Blenmore to a nonprofit corporation established to turn the home into a "social club for male wage earners and men of small income where such men shall have a place of resort, open to all well behaved men regardless of religious belief or political views; except that no person advocating the forcible overthrow of our constitutional government shall be entitled to the privileges of said club house." And so began the Charles F. Hamblen Club.

The Charles F. Hamblen House as it appears today. *Author's collection.*

Oral histories taken of those living and working in the town during the 1920s, 1930s and 1940s fondly recall the Hamblen Club (later to become American Legion Post 37) as a place where they could go to relax, have a drink, play cards, place bets and, in general, enjoy the same pursuits as the swells at the yacht club across the street, albeit on a less glamorous scale. And it was all thanks to Hamblen's concern for the common man. Or maybe it was a bit of yacht envy.

The Hamblen House was not limited to the Charles F. Hamblen Club. The corporation controlling the building also leased it out as a clubhouse for the Dewdrager (pronounced "Do drag her") Club, formed in 1921. (The club's theme song opens this chapter.) The Dewdragers were an invitation-only loosely organized association of young St. Augustinian men, most of whom were in their early twenties. Members were dedicated to hot jazz, plentiful alcohol (note that this was during Prohibition) and having as much "wicked" fun with beautiful young ladies as could be squeezed into their lives. The club members, many of whom went on to become city business leaders, kept meticulous accounting records for at least a portion of the club's existence, allowing a glimpse into their partying ways.

Club membership dues and entertainment assessments were regularly collected from the members. These funds, as well as fines collected for

The Hamblen House (gambling for the working man) and the St. Augustine Yacht Club (gambling for the super-rich) seen across the street from each other in this St. Augustine postcard dated 1904. *St. Augustine Historical Society.*

The Dewdrager's Ball, February 1936. *St. Augustine Historical Society.*

various infractions of club rules, paid for expenses incurred in the pursuit of good times. The Dewdragers regularly held dances—the "Dewdrager Balls" referred to in their theme song—as well as cookouts on St. Augustine's beaches and various dinners and suppers for the club members and their dates. Most recorded expenses are modest, ten to fifteen dollars on average for hall rental for dinners and dances, seven dollars for printed invitations, twenty to forty dollars for food.

The Dewdragers really show their dedication to the art of leisure activity, however, in the amounts they paid for music and liquid refreshment at their events. The costs for music range from a low of $20.00 ($259.00 in 2019 funds) to a whopping $225.00 ($2,913.78 in 2019) for the 1921 August Dewdragers Ball. The average amount spent, per event, for music was about $100.00 ($1,295.02 in 2019). That is *real* devotion to dancing. The expenditures for liquid refreshment, presumably alcoholic, were much more modest, ranging from $35.00 ($453.26) to $135.00 ($1,748.27). However, considering that during Prohibition most of the liquor was probably locally produced and could be purchased for anywhere between $1.00 and $60.00 *a gallon*, depending upon its aging and quality, the Dewdrager events appear to have been well fueled. Since membership in the club appears to have topped out at about thirty members, and event attendance was limited to the members and their dates, this worked out to a lot of booze per capita.

The Dewdragers Club lasted well into the 1930s in St. Augustine, but later revels paled in comparison to the blowouts of the early to mid-1920s. The Dewdragers got older and presumably more respectable—and they married respectable St. Augustine girls. The secretive earlier functions with their pricey musicians and abundant alcohol gave way to more staid events, wives included, that pictorially looked much like a high school prom. But for one shining moment, the Dewdragers epitomized "wicked" in St. Augustine.

There is one more stop on the wicked tour of the city proper. Across the plaza from the Hamblen House, on the side of the city south of King Street, at 213 Charlotte Street, sat the St. Augustine Tourist Club. If the Hamblen House was where the working-class St. Augustine resident went to gamble, the Tourist Club offered the same entertainments to the lower-income visitor who might have tired of carriage rides, picking oranges or gawking at alligators. Open to any man for a small initiation fee, here a member could purchase decent whiskey at an affordable price, by the glass or the bottle, wager at cards or indulge in off-track betting. With a number of brothels just a few doors away, this area of town was a cornucopia of delights for those out-of-towners with a budget to manage.

While the city of St. Augustine contained a good selection of working brothels and gambling facilities during the first half of the twentieth century, the true center of illegal entertainment lived just across the San Sebastián River up King Street—the Tomoka Road, as it was sometimes called.

GOOD TIMES INDEED– ST. AUGUSTINE'S ENTERTAINMENT SECTORS

New Augustine

From the late 1880s until the 1940s, the center of the prostitution industry in St. Augustine, as well as gambling and bootlegging, lay not in the city proper but just over the San Sebastián Bridge in New Augustine, now called West Augustine. During that period, all three industries were captained by Blanche Altavilla. Until now, Altavilla and her accomplishments have been little documented. But during the first half of the twentieth century, her Country Club was a well-known entertainment destination for the male population of the area, both resident and tourist.

The majority of arrests during this period for operating a house of ill fame (the term used in St. Augustine arrest records) are of landladies operating along King Street in New Augustine. Many of them were arrested multiple times, including Annie Wynn, Doris Shaw, May Harrel, Lizzie Fenell and Mable O'Conner, all of them operating within the Country Club perimeter. Margaret "Big Margaret" Norris, who owned the brothel adjacent to Blanche Altavilla's main residence, and Marie de Medici, whose first house was located at the northwest corner of what is now Leonardi Street and West King Street and later moved several blocks west to Blanche Altavilla's property, also suffered multiple arrests.

Blanche Travis (her name before her 1911 marriage to Sam Altavilla) started acquiring the land centering on what is now known as Blanche

Lane, Travis Place and Travis Lane in the 1880s, shortly after she arrived in St. Augustine. She began living and working at 262 West King Street in 1883. She acquired lots in the area from several sources, with the largest portion acquired in 1905 from Lawrence O. Davis and his wife for the then-substantial sum of $1,000 cash (about $29,101 in 2019 dollars). Blanche operated a brothel from this area as early as 1892—when court records show her first arrest as landlady of a house of ill repute—until the early 1950s.

In 1911, Blanche built her showplace, the Country Club, in the center of her property. This house is still standing today at her original 262 West King Street address. She lived in this house, operating her business and managing her property empire in that location, from 1911 until her death in December 1953.

Today, the house is owned by former city commissioner Arnett Chase. His family has operated the Chase Funeral Home from that location for over fifty years. The house was historically recognized as a center for civil rights activities in the 1960s. Although the interior of the house has been substantially altered since the days of its occupation by Blanche and her ladies, the bones are still there. What is now the sizable funeral home chapel was once divided into small bedroom spaces for the conduct of trade—the studs marking where the walls once stood remain visible in the flooring. Spaces still exist that were once elegant parlors and larger bedrooms for wealthier customers and for Blanche herself. The house contains the first modern bathroom facility installed in New Augustine—a small but adequate installation memorable because indoor plumbing was not common in St. Augustine until many decades later. Unconfirmed but rumored in the West Augustine community to this day is that when the attic was cleared out after Blanche's death in the 1950s, it contained a number of fixtures for the more sexually adventurous, including whips and bondage implements. The attic also supposedly held a lovely collection of fashionable women's shoes.

Blanche's house is only one of several that operated within the perimeter of the three streets encompassing the Country Club property. Operations continued for nearly seventy years—significantly longer than New Orleans's Storyville. The Country Club property was dedicated to the City of St. Augustine in 1941 by Blanche Altavilla and officially named the Altavilla Subdivision. Both prior to its dedication and afterward, until the 1950s, this property housed the cream of the area brothels, hosting not only the wealthy but also the middle- and lower-income clientele within its precincts.

It was billed as a one-stop entertainment district containing taverns, beer joints, billiard halls and gambling houses—all either owned by Blanche Altavilla outright or by people who worked for her under personal financial and business arrangements. These included brothels run by Margaret Norris at 266 West King Street (still standing today) and by Billie Burns at 16 Travis Place (building demolished in 2012) and a large tavern run by Mayme Colee located on Travis Place across from the Billie Burns house. The tavern is long gone, but the foundations of the building are still visible in the tall grass of the vacant lot. Today, many of the buildings, homes and cottages on the three streets bordering the Country Club, once used for illicit entertainment, are being renovated into modest suburban dwellings, probably inhabited by ghosts with amazing stories to tell.

In addition to the well-established Country Club, New Augustine appears to have been a revolving door for brothels that quickly came and went, probably because Blanche expeditiously sought out and absorbed her competition. Court records mention numerous establishments on West King Street, all of short duration. Others located on Live Oak Street and Whitney Street were run by landladies who eventually relocated to the Country Club precincts. The same is true for taverns, gambling houses and bootlegging operations.

The Country Club remained the epicenter of West Augustine for all of these activities, controlled by Blanche and her compatriots, including Sam Altavilla, who was known to produce an excellent moonshine. One of Blanche's female competitors in the liquor business, Annie Futch, operated from her home on Mackey Lane, just two blocks from Blanche's domain. In 1937, Annie pled no contest to selling whiskey without a license. In contrast to Blanche, who openly manufactured and sold liquor from the Country Club without any legal interference or penalty, Annie was sentenced to a $200 fine ($3,487 in 2019 dollars) and four months at hard labor in the county jail. Blanche had connections and knew how to deal with the opposition.

Another prominent local competitor in the moonshining business was the Stratton family, who lived near the San Sebastián River at 58 Florida Avenue. Rufus Stratton owned and operated the Stratton Tire Shop on King Street in the city of St. Augustine but, to support his family of eight children, also produced moonshine at several stills he operated in various locations in St. Johns County. Word is, Stratton's shine was some of the best in town. Cousin to the Oesterreichers of Palm Valley, also prominent

Rufus Stratton (*right*) after a deer hunt, 1930. Stratton was West Augustine's best-known bootlegger. *St. Augustine Historical Society.*

Bubba Stratton, Rufus Stratton's son, with alligator, 1954. *St. Augustine Historical Society.*

St. Johns County moonshiners, Stratton also employed Palm Valley's celebrated shine aging techniques, including using oak barrels, peaches, pears and palmetto berries to produce a superior, smooth-tasting product. Rufus's son Bubba recalled working the stills with his dad. He filled the gallon jugs with the initial 140-proof drippings from the still condensation coils and portioned out half pints, pints, quarts and gallons for sale to customers out of the six barrels of moonshine Rufus kept buried in the front yard of the Florida Avenue house.

The Stratton family's moonshine business thrived during Prohibition. Even St. Johns County sheriff E.E. Boyce was a satisfied customer. But as Prohibition came to a close in 1933, so did the Stratton liquor business. One

Hugie Oesterreicher and Rufus Stratton together in an undated photo. *St. Augustine Historical Society.*

day, federal revenue agents visited the tire shop and observed a half pint of Rufus's brew on his desk. The agents, aware of his business making and dealing shine, pointed out to him that they could arrest him for this violation of Prohibition, but to arrest him would cost too many federal dollars, have a negative impact on his family and, besides, with Prohibition ending, there was too much shine and too little profit to be had from the business anyway. Rufus agreed. In lieu of arrest for the half pint, he agreed to quit the liquor business. He traded one community service for another, joining the fire department instead.

LANDLADIES, GAMBLING, ALCOHOL AND THE LEGAL SYSTEM

*P*rostitution, gambling and the sale of alcohol were not only condoned and unlegislated during St. Augustine's early days but were also crucial to the maintenance of order in the colony, providing entertainment and release to what was then a largely male population. This remained the status quo for many decades, with these business enterprises largely confined to the city's ubiquitous taverns. The Spanish had a more relaxed attitude toward the more common vices, tolerating them in both the political and religious facets of life so long as they didn't lead to violence or general unrest.

St. Augustine had its share of drunken brawls and killings where the subject of dispute was a woman. Indeed, one of the apocryphal tales, told on nearly every ghost tour of the city, is that of Catalina Morain, a single and by all accounts attractive young woman ensconced in a large house on the bay front who ostensibly earned her living as a seamstress. Catalina had a number of admirers among the military men serving in St. Augustine, many of whom visited her on a regular basis. That is, they did until one blustery night in the fall of 1785 when a group of hooded men attacked and savagely knifed a suitor (or perhaps client) of Catalina's, one Lieutenant Guillermo Delaney of the Hibernian Regiment. The attack took place on Treasury Street, close to Catalina's residence at the end of the street near the bay front. Still alive, but mortally wounded, Delaney crawled to Catalina's house and collapsed on her doorstep. He survived long enough to give his statement to the local authorities, dying from his wounds some weeks afterward.

Catalina then became a focus of the investigation. She implicated two soldiers in the attack and was thought by some to be a person of interest, perhaps even soliciting the attack herself or providing its motive. The inquiry into the crime revealed that Catalina had many more admirers than Lieutenant Delaney and suggested that sewing for others was not the only service she provided to the public. Although it could not be proven that Catalina had any direct connection to Delaney's murder, she was jailed for four years for providing incorrect information to the authorities about potential suspects. Perjury warranted incarceration. Prostitution did not.

In 1821, as a result of treaty negotiations, the Spanish left town, and Florida (and, in consequence, St. Augustine) became a territory of the United States. The city became packed with young men seeking adventure and fortune in the new American lands. Amid all the debris, garbage and dilapidation left behind by the Spanish sprang up a surfeit of cheap boardinghouses, catering to the new bachelor population, who were more interested in womanizing, cockfighting, drinking and gambling than rebuilding a clean, safe and stable community.

Although the City of St. Augustine was always one to capitalize on the more wicked aspects of its citizens' appetites, two things happened in 1821 that put a decided damper on sin: First, the city council, a mixture of recently arrived Americans and Spanish/Menorcan residents who decided to stay in the newly proclaimed territory, resolved to raise money to clean up the mess in the city. Second, yellow fever invaded the city.

Yellow fever, also called "yellow jack," struck first. The first recorded death was that of Judge Thomas Fitch in July 1821; 172 other deaths quickly followed before the epidemic began to abate with the advent of cooler weather. Yellow fever did not discriminate. It felled the poor and the prominent equally, and among its victims were several of the city's physicians. Not knowing the cause of the disease ("effluvia" was suspected, but the real culprits were carrier mosquitoes breeding in the water collecting in the debris and garbage littering the town), residents kept to themselves and rarely ventured out after dark for fear of inhaling the bad air that they believed spread the disease. This fear and the constant and close presence of death certainly slowed the proliferation of sinful activities in the city as long as yellow fever was present.

Ultimately, the city council came to the realization that somehow the unsanitary condition of the city had something to do with the yellow fever epidemic and decided to do something about it. But first, the council needed money.

Since the most successful businesses were the operation of boardinghouses and the sale of liquor and the chief recreational activity of its citizens appeared to be "disorderly conduct," the council decided to do what governments usually do: tax, fine and license. Among the council's enactments in 1821: a $24.00 yearly tax on sellers of wine and spirits ($543.91 in 2019 dollars), plus 1 percent on the value of all stock in trade; a $50.00 ($1,133.15 in 2019) per year tax on each billiard table; and a $20.00 ($453.26 in 2019) annual tax on each boardinghouse or tavern.

Licenses in varying amounts were also required of those selling alcohol or operating boardinghouses, taverns or billiard halls, with a $20.00 fine levied for failure to have the correct license or for misuse of its terms. A nightly patrol of twenty-eight men was established to arrest "all disorderly persons found in the streets or making a riot or disturbance in any house or yard, and the said patrol are hereby authorized to enter any house or place where any tumult, riot or noise is made to the annoyance of the neighbors or disturbance of the tranquility of the city." Such disorderly persons were then fined the sum of $20.00. The number of men officially empowered to conduct the nightly patrols was remarkable in that the population of St. Augustine at this time did not exceed two thousand. Not all of the city's legal fundraising was based on its vices: dogs were also taxed, $2.00 ($45.33 in 2019) per year each.

The city didn't demand legislative action prohibiting its landladies, their employees and gambling and putting severe limitations on the purveyors of alcohol until toward the end of the Victorian era. Shortly before Henry Flagler announced his plans for remaking St. Augustine into a resort town for wealthy northern visitors and his purchase of large tracts of city land for that purpose, the city fathers decided that it would be prudent to officially curtail, at least in name, the entertainment businesses for which the city was famous.

On August 4, 1881, the City Board of Aldermen passed ordinances officially licensing dealers in alcoholic beverages and requiring them to pay the then-substantial license tax of $150.00 ($3,766.06 in 2019 dollars) for each place selling such beverages. On the same day, the aldermen also passed an ordinance "prohibiting houses of ill-fame, lewd or lascivious character to be kept or used within the City of St. Augustine."

The aldermen noted in their preface to this ordinance that its purpose was to establish "moral virtue" for the city, calling it necessary for the city's "advancement and prosperity" and for adding "stability to society and good government and security to its citizens." The ordinance established the fine for contravention of this ordinance at $10 per day, approximately $247 in 2019 currency, an amount that does not appear extraordinarily punitive or designed to stop the operation of what were then the most lucrative businesses in town. As a result, the brothels both in town and in New Augustine continued to thrive.

On April 13, 1886, the board of aldermen decided to extend its protection of the public morality by enacting another ordinance, this time suppressing gambling and gambling houses in St. Augustine. It now became a violation of law for anyone in the city to operate an establishment or even a room for the conduct or promotion of a lottery, dicing, numbers, games of chance, bunco, three-card monte or any other activity that implied the winning of money or articles of value dependent on those prohibited activities. The penalty for violation of this ordinance was $100 ($2,689 in 2019 currency) or sixty days in the city jail, at the discretion of the mayor.

Despite this legislation, such establishments as the Bacchus Club, the Zorayda Club and the Lorillard Villa still conducted high-stakes gambling and other entertainments on the floors above the ground floor of the exclusive men's restaurants and social clubs. Henry Flagler's well-heeled hotel guests and men of prominence and influence in the St. Augustine community frequented these clubs with impunity. During the Flagler years, there are no reports of raids or arrests ever made at these sites or at the Flagler hotels, and there were certainly no convictions of men of high reputation for patronizing either houses of ill repute or gambling establishments. Instead, these ordinances appear to have been created specifically to target the small-time hustlers and con men who populated the streets. These film-flam men set up their card tables on street corners to engage passersby in quick shell games, grabbing a few dollars before the police came around and prompted them to close up shop and move to the next corner. There were plenty of these arrests and convictions for this crime, lending credence to the belief that sin is tolerated a whole lot better if the sinner has a substantial bank account.

By 1895, the city ordinances regulating alcohol, gambling and the operation of brothels had been re-codified and expanded. Licensed dealers for the sale of alcohol could not engage in business in locations used for assignation or occupied by or frequented by women or in any location having or permitting instrumental music, phonographs or "like musical sound emitters"—a direct shot at the local brothels. Exceptions were made for keepers of public inns or hotels that provided food and lodging to the general public as a political courtesy to Flagler. Sale of alcohol to women and minors was strictly prohibited, as were Sunday sales. At this time, members of the city police force were, for the first time, legally prohibited from drinking alcohol on the job or from entering an establishment where alcoholic beverages were sold or where prostitution took place—except, of course, in the line of duty.

The 1895 revisions with regard to prostitution extended violations of law beyond ownership of houses of ill fame to anyone who was a "proprietor, manager, occupant, resident or frequenter" of a house of ill fame. For the first time in St. Augustine history, the law was made applicable not just to the madams and the prostitutes but also to their customers, although judging by the court records of the city, arrests and convictions of brothel customers were rare. Even arrests of the landladies and their working girls were uncommon. The majority of arrests occurred during election cycles when, presumably, incumbents felt compelled to demonstrate their commitment to the protection of public morals, at least until after Election Day, when business as usual resumed. The punishment for violation of any of the prostitution ordinances was in 1895 increased to a $100 ($2,605 in 2019 currency) fine or sixty days in the city jail.

In 1895, the law also expanded the definition of gambling to include gaming of any type with cards, any "wheel of fortune" or any mechanical device used for gambling, dice and the game of keno. The law designated that maintaining a house, room or other facility where gambling took place or where gaming devices were located was "operating a disorderly house" and was declared officially to be "dangerous to the peace and morals of the city." As with prostitution, violations of the gambling ordinances were punishable by a $100 fine or sixty days in jail. And as with prostitution, enforcement of these ordinances continued to be highly selective and in tandem with election cycles in the city. The roulette wheels at the Zorayda Club and the Lorillard Villa continued to turn.

On October 13, 1918, two full years before the January 17, 1920 effective date of the Eighteenth Amendment to the U.S. Constitution nationally prohibiting the sale of alcohol, the citizens of St. Augustine and St. Johns County took the extraordinary measure of voting to ban the sale and consumption of intoxicating spirits, wine and beer throughout the county, passing the law by a total of forty-five votes. This didn't seem to affect the status of alcohol consumption in the area, however, as the manufacture of liquor locally as well as its sale and consumption, in prodigious amounts, continued with the blessing and cooperation of politicians and law enforcement alike. This atmosphere of cooperation and mutual profit

Still, moonshine and illegal gambling equipment seized between Jacksonville and St. Augustine, date unknown. *Florida Memory.*

continued through Prohibition to the repeal of the Eighteenth Amendment on December 5, 1933, and through the decades that followed, up through the mid-1950s. It wasn't until consumption, production and importation of alcohol was legal *and* the price of commercially produced liquor made reasonable that St. Augustinians gave up their stills and went to the local package stores. But wait. Times they are a-changin' and St. Augustine has lately returned to the business of locally made liquor. Today at 112 Riberia Street, at what was once the city ice plant, you can pick up delectable spirits at the St. Augustine Distillery, including vodka, gin, rum and an award-winning bourbon, distilled on site from locally grown grains and sugar cane. At City Gates Spirits, 11 St. George Street, you can observe the distillation of flavored spirits, including moonshine, and sample (and purchase) the products made on site. At the San Sebastian Winery, located at 157 King Street in one of Henry Flagler's old East Coast Railway buildings, you can stock your cellar with fine wines, produced on site from Florida-grown muscadine grapes, as well as indulge in a vintage glass or two at the rooftop

Cellar Upstairs Wine, Jazz and Blues Bar. If a cold glass of locally brewed beer is your preference, St. Augustine offers many choices, including Dog Rose Brewing Company on Bridge Street, Old Coast Ales on Anastasia Boulevard, Ancient City Brewing Taproom on Cathedral Place, A1A Ale Works on King Street and West Augustine's pride, the Bog, on West King Street. From Pedro Menéndez's master brewer to today's experts in spirit distillation, St. Augustine boasts an unbroken line of alcohol production and consumption unique in American history.

Illustrative of the partnership between politics, law enforcement and prostitution in St. Augustine is the famous (or perhaps infamous) "Police Case," which enthralled the citizens in the summer of 1942. City hall was packed with lunch-toting spectators who wanted to take their minds off the daily horrors of war. For a brief time, the Police Case captured the biggest headlines in the *St. Augustine Record*, surpassing even the latest news about the Allied efforts in World War II. As previously noted, the *Record* rarely paid attention to matters involving prostitution and local corruption. The local attitude was that the seamier side of behavior just didn't take place in St. Augustine.

The Police Case began when two high-ranking officers of the St. Augustine Police Department—Police Chief William Lindsey and Captain Virgil Stuart—were summarily fired by the city administration led by Mayor Walter Fraser (also referred to by the landladies as the "Big Boss"). Fraser was known in the city for his tourist attractions, most notably the Fountain of Youth. The Fraser family still owns the Fountain of Youth today.

The men had allegedly accepted protection money from two popular St. Augustine brothels, to the tune of $3.00 ($46.50 in 2019 currency) per girl per week, plus other occasional payoffs of $100.00 ($1,550.00 in 2019 currency)—usually on holidays. They appealed their firing to the Civil Service Board. The ensuing hearings entertained St. Augustine for several weeks.

Witnesses included the two fired officers, several of the city's star landladies, the city tax assessor, the city manager, several city commissioners and the mayor himself. They painted a vivid picture of the interconnection between law enforcement and those breaking the law.

Among the more startling revelations was that Mayor Fraser had personally requested that three landladies—Blanche Altavilla, Margaret Norris and Billie Burns—sign affidavits prepared by his office accusing the fired officers of taking the protection money in question. The city tax assessor took the affidavits to the ladies for signature. The city tax

Above, left: Mayor Walter Fraser, the "Big Boss," of St. Augustine. *St. Augustine Historical Society.*

Above, right: Chief William Lindsey, St. Augustine police chief from 1934 to 1958. *St. Augustine Police Department.*

Left: Deputy Virgil Stuart, St. Augustine Police Department. *St. Augustine Historical Society.*

assessor testified that he was unaware of the ladies' occupation or the type of businesses they were conducting, that the ladies were personal friends of the mayor and under no political pressure to issue their affidavits and that the mayor had personally wanted to rid the police department of the officers in question.

Perhaps the most astonishing testimony came from Police Chief Lindsey, who denied taking any protection money, stating that there was no need to do so because the houses of prostitution in St. Augustine were under the direct supervision of the city sanitary department and the city police department. He further asserted that organized prostitution and gambling were well known and sanctioned by both the city commission and the city administration. He also stated that he had been instructed by the mayor to look the other way when it came to prostitution, gambling and even the Sunday liquor laws because of the city's status as a tourist town and its economic dependence on those activities. The mayor had declared to him that these laws existed "for the preachers' benefit," but no one was actually expected to comply with them.

Chief Lindsey also noted that one of the city commissioners, Charles Peters, operated an illegal gambling facility and the city commission knew about it. In later testimony, City Manager Ray Wilson testified that enforcement (or lack thereof) of the laws regarding illegal sale of liquor on Sundays, gambling and the operation of houses of prostitution were carried out "in accordance with the wishes of the city commission."

The ultimate result of this byzantine account of corruption, money, politics and sin in St. Augustine was that the Civil Service Board found that the accusations against the fired officers were without foundation and that they were "not guilty and completely exonerated" from charges of accepting graft. The board also directed the city to immediately reinstate the two officers in their former positions at the police department and to compensate the two men for all owed back pay. The brothels in West Augustine suspended operations for a short while during the hearings, but once the decision was reached by the board in late June 1942, business went back to normal, continuing without note in the St. Augustine press until the early 1950s and the deaths of the town's preeminent landladies.

THE END OF CITY TRADITIONS

*I*n the early 1950s, with the end of World War II and the beginning of a new age of prosperity in the postwar days, the prostitution industry of St. Augustine began to change. Most importantly, the status of women had improved significantly. Women were entitled to be educated and could hold jobs sufficient to support themselves and their families without social reproach. Occupations and professions previously closed were now open to them. Prostitution was no longer the economic imperative it had been. As the decade progressed and the 1960s loomed, attitudes about the sexual independence of women also began to change. Casual sex became less of a business and more of a pastime. Paying for sex was not as necessary when sex outside of marriage for individuals was no longer the societal kiss of death it had once been. And the landladies who had so successfully managed and controlled the sex trade in St. Augustine for nearly half a century were either dying or moving on.

Ocie Martin was the first to go, dying in her forties in 1933 from "nephritis and erysipelas," according to her death certificate. Billie Burns, after nearly a decade of operating her own house within the Blanche Altavilla Country Club precincts, closed up and left town for parts unknown in 1938. Margaret Norris retired in the late 1950s, choosing to return to North Carolina where she was said to have spent her childhood and where she still had family. Blanche Altavilla died in 1953 at the age of ninety-three, one of the town's wealthiest women. With her passing, so did the age of organized brothels in St. Augustine.

Some quiet rejoicing likely broke out among some residents of St. Augustine at the demise of the brothels. St. Augustine could now truly, with a straight face, promote itself as the family-friendly destination that Henry Flagler had touted all along. Surprisingly, a number of old-timers from distinguished families had a different opinion.

Under the landladies' control (and with the cooperation of city and county government), prostitution had been properly regulated. The girls were healthy, received regular medical attention and had few illegitimate births resulting from their work. St. Augustine residents who were interviewed in the late 1970s and early 1980s said the girls who worked in these brothels were mostly well mannered and well dressed and were not considered "low-class."

With the closing of the brothels, however, prostitution moved into the streets, well outside of the city proper and its environs. It became associated with drug use, violent crime, increased incidence of sexually transmitted diseases and increased numbers of children born out of wedlock. In the opinion of one matron, closing the brothels was the worst thing that ever happened to the moral and social condition of St. Augustine. The rejoicing that came with the end of that form of immorality came at a high cost.

As for the city's preoccupation with alcohol consumption, nothing much has changed. Alcohol may now be produced and consumed legally, as long as the licensing laws are observed and those who choose to imbibe don't get behind the wheel of a car.

Prohibitions against gambling seem to ebb and flow in Florida. Anyone over the age of eighteen can now purchase a state lottery ticket or play blackjack at any one of a number of Seminole tribe–owned casinos in the state. Wagering on horses and jai alai games continues unabated, although greyhound racing recently met its end thanks to a Florida constitutional amendment. Technology and access to the internet allow anyone with the desire to gamble to do so from the comfort of home.

What used to be characterized as good old-fashioned sin is now categorized as an addiction—to alcohol, gambling or sex—and as a disease or character disorder to be treated and cured. Wickedness, as it was defined in earlier, simpler times is now barely recognized as iniquitous, having been supplanted by the greater-in-scope evils of corporate greed, widespread political corruption and destruction of the environment.

Organized prostitution, bootlegging and gambling were nothing if not hallowed traditions in the Oldest City for close to four hundred years,

Having a hot time in old Fort Marion, 1905. Booze, oysters and loose women partying in a dungeon at the Castillo de San Marcos, formerly known as Fort Marion, St. Augustine. *St. Augustine Historical Society.*

contributing to the city's economy and stability as well as to its reputation as an entertainment venue. Times change. But St. Augustine is defined by its celebration of its past. Do not forget its citizens who, by promoting and managing the city's celebrated vices, contributed so much to its character.

BIBLIOGRAPHY

*St. Augustine Historical Society

Note on Flagler

Graham, Thomas. "Flagler's Grand Hotel Alcazar." *El Escribano* 24 (1989).
———. *Mr. Flagler's St. Augustine.* Gainesville: University Press of Florida, 2014.

Chapter 1

Bushnell, Amy. "The Expenses of *Hidalguia* in Seventeenth-Century St. Augustine." *El Escribano* 15 (1978).
City of St. Augustine papers files. MC-19, Boxes 1, 2, and 4. SAHS.*
Copy of a Plan of the City of St. Augustine, Florida, with additions for the year 1883. SAHS.
Cuisine, James G. "Hello Sailor! St. Augustine as a Seaport, 1784–1800." *El Escribano* 47 (2010).
Deagan, Kathleen A. "The Archeology of First Spanish Period of St. Augustine." *El Escribano* 15 (1978).
Enlarged reproduction of City Blocks from the de la Roque map of 1778. SAHS.

Gordon, Elsbeth. "So Precious a Watering." *El Escribano* 43 (2006).

Graham, Thomas. *Mr. Flagler's St. Augustine.* Gainesville: University Press of Florida, 2014.

Griffin, Patricia C. *Mullet on the Beach, the Minorcans of Florida, 1768–1788.* Gainesville: University Press of Florida, 1991.

Hoffman, Kathleen S. "The Material Culture of Seventeenth-Century St. Augustine." *El Escribano* 32 (1995).

Lawson, Edward. "Translation of Letters of Pedro Menendez de Aviles and Other Documents Relative to His Career, 1555–1574." SAHS.

Lowery, Woodbury. *The Spanish Settlements Within the Present Limits of the United States, Florida, 1562–1574.* New York, 1959.

Lyon, Eugene. *The Enterprise of Florida: Pedro Menendez de Aviles and the Spanish Conquest of 1565–1568.* Gainesville: University Press of Florida, 1976.

———. "Richer Than We Thought—Appendix B: Personal Property Inventories: Sixteenth Century Soldiers and Sailors." *El Escribano* 29 (1992).

———. "St. Augustine 1580—The Living Community." *El Escribano* 14 (1977).

Chapter 2

Cuisine, James G. "Hello Sailor! St. Augustine as a Seaport, 1784–1800." *El Escribano* 47 (2010).

Enlarged reproduction of City Blocks from the de la Roque Map of 1788. SAHS.

Graham, Thomas. *The Awakening of St. Augustine, the Anderson Family and the Oldest City, 1821–1924.* St. Augustine, FL: St. Augustine Historical Society, 1978.

Griffin, John W. "St. Augustine in 1822." *El Escribano* 14 (1977).

Griffin, Patricia. "Mary Evans: Woman of Substance." *El Escribano* 14 (1977).

Landers, Jane. *Black Society in Spanish Florida.* Chicago: University of Illinois Press, 1999.

Plan of the City of St. Augustine based on a map by Mariano LaRoque and his accompanying description, dated April 25, 1788. SAHS.

Swanson, Russell. "Social Welfare at Work During the Second Spanish Colonial Period in St. Augustine." 1988. MC-21. SAHS.

Chapter 3

Altavilla, Blanche. Death Certificate. Bureau of Vital Statistics, State of Florida.

———. Last Will and Testament. Probate Records, St. Johns County, Florida.

Altavilla, Mayme. Death Certificate. Bureau of Vital Statistics, State of Florida.

Altavilla, Salvatore. Death Certificate. Bureau of Vital Statistics, State of Florida.

———. Immigration, Citizenship and Enlistment records. United States of America.

Anonymous. Oral history interview conducted by the author in St. Augustine, FL, March 19, 2017.

———. Oral history interview conducted by the author in St. Augustine, FL, February 3, 2019.

Bland and Associates Inc. "The West Augustine Historic District Assessment Survey, City of St. Augustine, St. Johns County, Florida." Prepared for the St. Johns Board of County Commissioners, June 2008.

Census Records. 1920–1950. State of Florida and United States of America.

Chase, Arnett. Oral history interview conducted by the author in St. Augustine, FL, on June 11, 2018.

City of St. Augustine cemetery records. SAHS.

Colee family papers. SAHS.

Colonel Louis Bell papers. SAHS.

Graham, Thomas. "Flagler's Grand Hotel Alcazar." *El Escribano* 24 (1989).

Griffin, Patricia C., and Diana Selsor Edwards. Edited by Robert Nawrocki. "Richard Twine: A Brief Biography." *El Escribano* 53 (2016).

Hotel file. SAHS.

Hugas, Mario, and Madeline Hugas. Oral history interview conducted by Robert McDaniel in St. Augustine, FL, on May 5, 1981. Oral history tape B-56. SAHS.

Johnson, Benjamin Franklin. Oral history interview conducted by Carrie Johnson in St. Augustine, FL in 1999. Oral history tapes A-136 and B-136. SAHS.

Light, Chad. "A Walk Through History, 150 Years of Lincolnville." *Old City Life* 2, no. 2 (February 2017).

Martin, Ocie. Death Certificate. Bureau of Vital Statistics, State of Florida.

Mayor's Court Records, City of New Augustine, St. Johns County, Florida. SAHS.

Mohlman, Geoffrey. "Lincolnville—An Anthropological History of Black St. Augustine." 1991. SAHS.

Property Appraiser's Records, St. Johns County, Florida.

Property Records, 1820-1965, St. Johns County, Florida.

Richard Twine Photograph Collection. SAHS.

St. Augustine City Directories, R.L. Polk and Company, 1888–1966.

St. Augustine Herald. August 25, 1899.

St. Johns County Court Case Collection, civil cases, St. Johns County Circuit Court. SAHS.

St. Johns County Court Case Collection, criminal cases, St. Johns County Circuit Court. SAHS.

Sanborn Fire Insurance Maps of Florida, City of St. Augustine, #4, 5, 7, 10, 20, 22, 23, 24 and 28.

The Tatler. January 27, 1894.

Vickers, Barbara. "The Heart of Lincolnville." *El Escribano* 43 (2006).

Wilder, Robert. *God Has a Long Face.* New York: G.P. Putnam's Sons, 1940.

Chapter 4

Anonymous. Oral history interview conducted by the author in St. Augustine, Florida, on June 14, 2019

Carter, Greg. Oral history interview conducted by the author in St. Augustine, Florida, on July 2, 2019.

Colee, Charles. Oral history interview conducted by Thomas Graham in St. Augustine, Florida, on March 17, 1976. Oral history tape B-45. SAHS.

Davis, Sheriff L.O. Oral history interview conducted by Frankie Walker in St. Augustine, Florida, Date unknown. Oral history tapes B-75, 1 and 2. SAHS.

Florida Herald. "A Temperance Society." November 18, 1830.

Green, David B. Oral history interview conducted by Craig Burdick in St. Augustine, Florida, on April 29, 1977. Oral history tapes B42 and B43. SAHS.

Hall, Maggie, and the St. Augustine Historical Society. Images of America: *St. Augustine.* Charleston, SC: Arcadia Publishing, 2002.

Hotel File. SAHS.

Howells, William Dean. "A Confession of St. Augustine." *El Escribano* 35 (1998).

Hugas, Mario, and Madeline Hugas. Oral history interview conducted by Robert McDaniel in St. Augustine, Florida, on May 5, 1981. Oral history tape B-56. SAHS.

Johnson, Benjamin Franklin. Oral history interview conducted by Carrie Johnson in St. Augustine, Florida, in 1999. Oral history tapes A-136 and B-136. SAHS.

Little, Mark, ed. "Childhood Memories." *El Escribano* 44 (2007).

Manucy, William H. Jr. Oral history interview conducted by Albert Manucy in St. Augustine, Florida, on October 28, 1970. Oral history tape B-15. SAHS.

Map of St. Johns County, St. Johns County GIS, 2019.

Masters, Earl. Oral history interview conducted by Mrs. John Kessler in St. Augustine, Florida, on April 28, 1977. Oral history tape B-47. SAHS.

Mickler family papers. SAHS.

Mickler, Flavian. Oral history interview conducted by Frankie Walker in St. Augustine, Florida, on July 16, 1991. Oral history tape B-95. SAHS.

Oesterreicher, Michel. *Pioneer Family.* Tuscaloosa: University of Alabama Press, 1996.

Property Appraiser's Records, St. Johns County, Florida.

Property Records, St. Johns County, Florida.

St. Augustine Evening Record. "Booze! Booze! Booze!" October 12, 1917.

———. Grape juice advertisement. October 17, 1917.

———. "Local Saloons Close Tonight." September 29, 1917.

———. "Man Was Beaten by Gang." December 9, 1922.

———. "Opium. Smoking in a Chinese Laundry." November 29, 1902.

———. "Package Houses Must Remove Stocks." October 22, 1917.

———. "Sheriff Captures Stills." November 12, 1922.

———. "St. Johns County Now in Dry List." October 15, 1917.

———. "36 States Have Ratified the Nation-Wide Amendment." January 19, 1919.

———. "Two Alleged Moonshiners." January 16, 1920.

———. "Went for Prohibition." October 14, 1917.

St. Augustine Record. "Capture of 500 Gallon Still." February 10, 1936.

———. "Capture of Largest Still." August 14, 1926.

———. "Capture of Still on Fish Island." March 11, 1933.

———. "Capture of Two Large Copper Stills." January 26, 1937.

———. "Increasing Visits of Coast Guard Cutters." September 11, 1926.

———. "JAM: Drugs and the Community." January 15, 1973.

———. "Liquor Pirates." August 8, 1926.

———. "Liquor Ran Like Water." August 7, 1926.

———. "Moonshine Business Kept Local Police Busy." March 12, 2012.

———. "Moonshine Captured in Crescent Beach." October 7, 1938.

———. "Moonshine Still at Moccasin Branch." September 28, 1958.

———. "Seizure of the *Paloma*." June 24, 1926.

———. "Sheriff Boyce Still On the Hunt." November 7, 1936.

———. "Shine Still Raided." August 29, 1970.

———. "Still Found on SR 16." December 28, 1938.

———. "Still Seized at Julington Creek." May 10, 1939.

St. Johns County Court Case Collection, civil cases, St. Johns County Circuit Court. SAHS

St. Johns County court Case Collection, criminal cases, St. Johns County Circuit Court. SAHS.

Typed reminiscences of an unknown person about life in St. Augustine, 1885. MC-21. SAHS.

Chapter 5

Bacchus Club file. SAHS

Belmont, Ann L. "The St. Augustine Yacht Club." July 1978. SAHS.

Carter, Greg. Oral history interview conducted by the author in St. Augustine, Florida, on July 2, 2019.

City Directory, St. Augustine, 1907.

Colee, Charles. Oral history interview conducted by Thomas Graham in St. Augustine, Florida, on March 17, 1976. Oral history tape B-45. SAHS.

Florida Times-Union. "Inaugural Race." March 23, 1889.

———. "Yacht Club House Sold." October 18, 1925.

Florida Times-Union and Journal. "Rooster Fighting." November 11, 1973.

Graham, Thomas. *Mr. Flagler's St. Augustine*. Gainesville: University Press of Florida, 2014.

Green, David B. Oral history interview conducted by Craig Burdick in St. Augustine, Florida, on April 29, 1977. Oral history tapes B-42 and B-43. SAHS.

Harvey, Karen. *Legends and Tales: Remembering St. Augustine*. Charleston, SC: The History Press, 2006.

Hugas, Mario, and Madeline Hugas. Oral history interview conducted by Robert McDaniel in St. Augustine, Florida, on May 5, 1981. Oral history tape B-56. SAHS.

Johnson, Benjamin Franklin. Oral history interview conducted by Carrie Johnson in St. Augustine, Florida, in 1999. Oral history tapes A-136 and B-136. SAHS.

Keys, Leslee F. *Hotel Ponce de Leon.* Gainesville: University Press of Florida, 2015.

Letter from the Association for the Preservation of Gamefowl to Charles Tingley, St. Augustine Historical Society, April 15, 1996.

Manucy, William H. Jr. Oral history interview conducted by Albert Manucy in St. Augustine, Florida, on October 28, 1970. Oral history tape B-15. SAHS.

Masters, Earl. Oral history interview conducted by Mrs. John Kessler in St. Augustine, Florida, on April 28, 1977. Oral history tape B-47. SAHS.

Matthews, Frank. Oral history interview conducted by Henry Johns in St. Augustine, Florida, on May 7, 1977. Oral history tape B-62. SAHS.

Mickler, Flavian. Oral history interview conducted by Frankie Walker in St. Augustine, Florida, on July 16, 1991. Oral history tape B-95. SAHS.

Property Appraiser's Records, St. Johns County, Florida.

Property Records, 1820-1965, St. Johns County, Florida

Raisz, Erwin, and Associates. *Atlas of Florida.* Gainesville: University Press of Florida, 1964.

St. Augustine Record. "Billiards: a St. Augustine Game Since 1565." February 28, 1991.

———. "Drifting Back into Ancient City History." June 28, 1998.

———. "Fire Damages Old Structure." January 18, 1939.

———. "Five Persons Arrested at Cockfights Here." March 20, 1966.

———. "Old City Site of State's First Yacht Club." February 20, 1988.

———. "Plans for County Harness Racing Track." December 21, 1952.

St. Johns County Court Case Collection, civil cases, St. Johns County Circuit Court. SAHS

St. Johns County Court Case Collection, criminal cases, St. Johns County Circuit Court. SAHS.

The Tatler. "Chit-Chat". January 19, 1895.

———. "St. Augustine Yacht Club." February 3, 1894.

———. "St. Augustine Yacht Club." January 25, 1896.

Vogeler, Edward Jerome. "Cock Fighting in Florida." SAHS.

Vollbrecht, John L. "The St. Augustine Yacht Club." SAHS.

The Wonderer. MC-63. SAHS.

Chapter 6

Anonymous. Oral history interview conducted by the author in St. Augustine, Florida, on March 19, 2017.

Anonymous. Oral history interview conducted by the author in St. Augustine, Florida, on February 3, 2019.

Bacchus Club file. SAHS.

Dewdragers Club file. SAHS.

Folioweekly. "Post Mortem." January 16, 2001.

Graham, Thomas. *Mr. Flagler's St. Augustine.* Gainesville: University Press of Florida, 2014.

Hamblen, Charles F. Last Will and Testament. Probate Records, St. Johns County, Florida.

Keys, Leslee F. *Hotel Ponce de Leon.* Gainesville: University Press of Florida, 2015.

Manucy, Joseph Herman Jr. Oral history interview conducted by Albert Manucy in St. Augustine, Florida, on November 4, 1970. Oral history tape B-17. SAHS.

1911–1915 Photograph album #12, Volumes A, B, and C. Box 2. SAHS.

Parker, Susan Richbourg. "Golfing, Fishing and Politics: President Harding's Visits to St. Augustine." *El Escribano* 46 (2009).

Property Appraiser's Records, St. Johns County, Florida.

Property Records, St. Johns County, Florida.

Sanborn Fire Insurance Maps of Florida, City of St. Augustine, #4, 5, 7, 10, 20, 22, 23, 24 and 28.

St. Augustine City Directories, R.L. Polk and Company, 1886–1966.

St. Augustine Record. "Battle on the Bayfront." September 29, 2000.

Westbrook, John. Oral history interview conducted by Albert Manucy in St. Augustine, Florida, on January 31, 1971. Oral history tape B-31. SAHS.

Chapter 7

Chase, Arnett. Oral history interview conducted by the author in St. Augustine, Florida, on June 11, 2018.

Little, Mark, ed. "Childhood Memories." *El Escribano* 44 (2007).

Property Appraiser's Records, St. Johns County, Florida.

Property Records, St. Johns County, Florida.

Sanborn Fire Insurance Maps of Florida, City of St. Augustine, #4, 5, 7, 10, 20, 22, 23, 24 and 28.

St. Augustine City Directories, R.L. Polk and Company, 1886–1966.

St. Johns County Court Case Collection, criminal cases, St. Johns County Circuit Court. SAHS.

West Augustine Oral History Project. SAHS.

Chapter 8

Colee Family papers. SAHS.

Edwards, Virginia. *Stories of Old St. Augustine.* St. Augustine, FL: Historic Print and Map Company, 2005.

Griffin, John W. "St. Augustine in 1822." *El Escribano* 14 (1977).

Harvey, Karen. *Daring Daughters, St. Augustine's Feisty Females, 1565–2000.* Virginia Beach, VA: Donning Company, 2002.

Lyon, Eugene. "St. Augustine 1580: The Living Community." *El Escribano* 14 (1977).

Map of St. Augustine, 1845. SAHS.

St. Augustine City Ordinance files. MC-17, Box 4. SAHS.

St. Johns County Court Case Collection, civil cases, St. Johns County Circuit Court. SAHS.

St. Johns County Court Case Collection, criminal cases, St. Johns County Circuit Court. SAHS.

Chapter 9

Little, Mark, ed. "Childhood Memories." *El Escribano* 44 (2007).

Probate Records, St. Johns County, Florida.

St. Augustine City Directories, R.L. Polk and Company, 1886–1966.

ABOUT THE AUTHOR

 nn Colby has been a Florida resident since 1960. She grew up in Orlando, attended the University of Florida, received her bachelor's degree in religion in 1973 and graduated from the University of Florida Law School in 1976. After serving as a local government counsel for forty-two years in the Central Florida area, she retired in 2016 with her husband, Bill MacLeod, to St. Augustine, a city she visited many times over the course of her life in Florida. She now spends her time doing historical research on arcane topics, working for Central Florida Pug Rescue, acting as a tour guide to the many northern friends and relatives who visit her and otherwise doing exactly as she pleases.

Visit us at
www.historypress.com

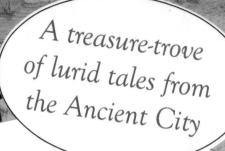

A treasure-trove of lurid tales from the Ancient City

When Pedro Menéndez de Avilés founded St. Augustine in 1565, his New World survival kit included gambling, liquor and ladies for hire. For the next four hundred years, these three industries were vital in keeping the city financially afloat. With the cooperation of law enforcement and politicians, St. Augustine's madams, bootleggers and high-rollers created a veritable Riviera where tourists, especially the wealthy, could indulge in almost every vice and still bring the family along for a wholesome vacation picking oranges and gawking at alligators. Join historian Ann Colby's tour of spots not on the standard tourist map to discover hidden-in-plain-sight bordellos, speakeasies, casinos and the occasional opium den.

THE History PRESS